ARAN ISLANDS

ARAN ISLANDS
A Personal Journey

By Dennis Smith

Photographs by Bill Powers

DOUBLEDAY & COMPANY, INC., GARDEN CITY, NEW YORK

1980

DESIGNED BY LAURENCE ALEXANDER

Library of Congress Cataloging in Publication Data
Smith, Dennis, 1940-
Aran Islands.
1. Aran Islands—Description and travel.
2. Smith, Dennis, 1940-   I. Powers, Bill.
II. Title.
DA990.A8S64   941.7′48
ISBN: 0-385-13591-2
Library of Congress Catalog Card Number 77-25609
Text Copyright © 1980 by Dennis Smith
Photographs Copyright © 1980 by Bill Powers

For our children
Brendan, Dennis, Sean, Deirdre, and Aislinn Smith,
and
Michael and Jimmy Powers.

ACKNOWLEDGMENTS

I would like to thank Mrs. O'Flaherty, Mrs. Mulkerrins, and Mrs. Conneely of the Aran Islands, for their graciousness and warm hospitality; my editors, Patrick Filley and Lindy Hess, for their enthusiasm; the crew of the M.S. *Naomh Eanna* and the Aer Arann pilots for their safe and amiable transportation; Bord Fáilte (Irish Tourist Board) and Aer Lingus for their great and cooperative spirit, particularly Sean Carberry and Tom Kennedy.

And Bill Powers, without whom this book would be incomplete, has my unending appreciation.

ARAN ISLANDS

THERE ARE three small rocks in the Atlantic Ocean, thirty miles west of Galway City, toward Boston, called the Aran Islands. Like a blessed barrier reef protecting holy Ireland, they stand up from the sea, defiant in their isolation, proud even in their uniqueness. If they are anything, they are isolated and unique. Scholars the world over, like pilgrams, trek to Aran to rub the limestone of a windswept geology, to search the mounds of Iron Age burials, to imagine a history that has not been recorded, to listen, finally, to the waves and the soft voices speaking in a nearly forgotten language. They come as far as from Japan.

"There are no scholars in Japan," I once heard a Dublin journalist say, "as there are no writers in America." But the Aran Islands are as removed from Dublin as they are from Mecca, and the bittersweet words floated unanswered in the dead barroom air of Irish journalism.

A pilgrim's search may be ironic, but a pilgrim never searches for irony. His travel is inspired by an internal belief in something, mundane or supernatural, a quest for knowledge or blessing or both. His reward is the memory of having been there.

The sky was dark this morning, and as I walked to the Galway pier I could hear the wind's melody passing through the city and across Galway Bay toward the Aran Islands. It was a brisk morning, chilled and wet-aired.

The ship to Aran is called the *Naomh Eanna,* Irish for St. Enda, the son of a fifth-century Druid chieftain, who founded a monastery on the big island. The ship is old—its decks of splintering wood—and is made for perhaps two hundred people. It seemed to be full this morning, with Irish-speakers—islanders, I thought, laden with cardboard boxes from Galway shopping—and with tourists, Nikons hanging from their necks like Olympic medals.

After buying a ticket from a man in a ramshackle hut at the pier's edge, I boarded the *Naomh Eanna,* carrying one suitcase and a canvas picnic bag filled with books and two writing pads, and wandered through the crowd until I found a coil of thick rope on the aft end of the deck. I sat there, waiting for the boat to depart, and began to read a biography of Synge.

The Irish playwright John Millington Synge (pronounced "sing") first went to the Aran Islands at W. B. Yeats's urging in 1898. He had been in Paris, unhappy and unproductive, and Yeats assured him of an awakening in the west of Ireland, amid the folkways of a people made poor by rocks but made rich in language by the hardships of isolation.

The Aran Islands are thirty miles to the southwest of Galway City, just five miles northwest of the Cliffs of Moher in County Clare, and just six miles south of the coastline islands of Connemara. The largest of the Arans, Inishmore (Inis Mór, in Irish), is about eight miles long by two wide, comprising 7,635 acres. (It is sometimes called "Aranmore.") Inishmore is the only one of the three Aran Islands accessible by large craft. The middle island, Inishmaan (Inis Meáin) is three miles long by two wide, comprising 2,252 acres. The smallest island, Inisheer (Inis Oirr) is nearly round in appearance and comprises 1,400 acres. In further translation they would be called the Big Island, the Middle Island, and the East Island.

These three rock ledges are world famous, having fired the imagination of international audiences through the dark frames of Robert Flaherty's 1934 film, *Man of Aran*, and before that through the genius and the magic of Synge's writing.

Between 1898 and 1901 Synge visited the islands four times. His longest stay was for six weeks, but in those short periods he felt as if he were "beyond the dwelling place of man," in "a world of inarticulate power." He was a natural romantic, and as Byron found Greece, Synge found Aran, and from his experiences here he wrote a diary, *The Aran Islands* (1907), and the play *Riders of the Sea* (1904). Two other plays, *In the Shadow of the Glen* (1904) and *The Playboy of the Western World* (1907), were taken from stories he had heard while living on Inishmaan.

These works, which tell the story of a natural, courageous people, have given me much pleasure, and as there are Shavians, Joyceans, and Yeatsians abundant in this world, I set about to add a humble voice to a small group of people who sing praises of Synge. I went to Aran, for it is the Syngian's baptism to make the pilgrimage, to see life as Synge saw it, to live it, perhaps, as he lived it. But, I wondered as the boat began to steam away from Galway, was that still possible?

When Synge first boarded a steamer for the Aran Islands in 1898, the crossing was completed in three hours. It takes as long today as it took three quarters of a century ago. There is an eight-passenger airplane to Inishmore each morning, at least during the tourist season, but I determined to travel as Synge did, a determination I would little advise others, for it can be an uneasy journey.

After an hour out to sea, beneath the black, racing clouds, the ship began to roll and pitch like, it seemed, a small toy on the surface of a whirlpool bath. Many of the passengers, even the experienced islanders, became seasick and hung over the side like beaten veterans, bewailing each wave. I continued to sit on the coil of rope, drinking strong black tea from a paper cup, trying to hold flat the wind-blown pages of my book. But the sea became too great a challenge to the sedentary and peaceful demands of reading, so I closed the book, moved to the bow of the boat, and awaited the islands. The full pushing of the wind against me felt cleansing, and though cold and wet I stayed there, awaiting the adventure that had been promised me by books and dreams.

The islands finally appeared, first as vague outlines through the mist, like a Seurat painting, and then clearer and clearer as the ship rushed on.

We stopped first at Inisheer, the small east island, anchoring a hundred yards from shore, while canvas-covered curraghs (pronounced "curracks") oared toward us like swimming bugs. The small craft were steadied in the splashing water by weatherworn young men pulling on strange sticks called *modjee-raw,* oars that are the same width, about four inches, at both ends. I saw a crowd of islanders standing on the shore, either waiting for parcels or perhaps simply taking in the small entertainment of diversion. We anchored next off Inishmaan, the Middle Island, where, besides the supply boxes, two passengers also left the boat, speaking in their native language. There seemed to be no pause between their words, and the intonation range was greater than in any language I've heard, more a vocalese than a songful chant. Again, there were many islanders gathered on the shore line to watch the activity.

Here, a curragh pulled a cow through the water, the animal swimming naturally enough but quietly, too pusillanimous to moo. A hoist was lowered from the deck and tied to a cinch that had been strapped around the animal's belly, and it was lifted out of the water. There is no other way to transport cattle from the smaller islands, but the whole procedure would make an SPCA official cringe, I think.

The ship finally docked at Kilronan, the pier town of Inishmore, the Big Island, but there were surprisingly few villagers waiting as on the smaller islands. There were twenty or so horse-pulled carts, their drivers hawk-ing an hour's sightseeing ride to the tourists who had come out just for the day. It reminded me of the children's pony ride in Central Park in New York. All tourists, I thought, are like children.

I asked one red-faced driver if he would take me to Mrs. O'Flaherty's house in Oat Quarter. He grumbled a little, for there would be no return trip, but nodded his head in consent. I climbed into the back of the cart. I did not speak then, for as the cart progressed I became immediately preoccupied—nearly hypnotized—by the unending, ubiquitous rock walls about me. Hundreds of them, shooting off in all directions.

As there are stars in the sky there are silver-gray stones on Inishmore.

After four miles of progressive climbing, the horse finally stopped in front of Aras Bhrid (Bridget's House), the O'Flaherty house. I paid the driver. Mrs. O'Flaherty came from the house, a woman of fifty or fifty-five perhaps, keen-eyed and smiling. Wiping her hands on an apron, she welcomed me.

"Is it Dennis Smith?" she asked.

It was, I told her.

"You were due here yesterday," she said in soft reprimand. "Come in now, and I'll give you some tongue."

I thought she meant a meal and I was not at all hungry. I followed her into the two-story, concrete-washed house, thinking up an apology to refuse the food, until she sat me down, whereupon I realized it was a tongue-lashing she meant.

I had spent an extra day in Galway and was arriving a day late.

"I have a telephone, you know," she said. There are now more than eighty telephones on this island, which has a population just over nine hundred.

I should have called from Galway, and I regretted that I had not. I told her so, and she smiled. "I'm giving out to you," she said, "and I only give out to people I like." "Tongue" and "giving out" are synonymous on these islands. She was a kind woman, and I had the feeling I would want to kiss her when I left.

In the house I found the O'Flahertys speak Irish in conversation. Mrs. O'Flaherty explained that English was her second language, and she apologized for any mistakes she might make. I said, "I'd bet you can't remember the last time you made a mistake in English." Pleased by that, she laughed. I was then shown to my room, where I sat for a while, reading. Afterward I took a walk down the road.

I walked for more than a mile until I could see, on a high hill, Dún Aengus, an ancient fortress. When Christ was born in Bethlehem, a fierce group of Belgic Celts were wrestling stones on the Aran Islands. It is historical speculation to say where these people came from, for no record is written of them. It is sure, though, that they were adventurers and fish eaters, perhaps a beaten tribe from the mainland searching for an impregnable shelter.

Unlike the Egyptians, they left behind them bare monuments like this Dún Aengus—just great walls, mortarless, and in places more than twelve feet thick, built on the edge of a three-hundred-foot cliff overlooking the sea that cannot rest.

The outer rampart, containing a middle rampart, an inner rampart, and the fort, encloses eleven acres. The inner rampart in places is eighteen feet high and nearly thirteen feet thick.

Truly a bastion set against unclimbable cliffs, Dún Aengus must have been a formidable defense against plunderers and land-hungry raiders, for even today's peace-loving tourist must approach the fort with a slow and careful climb.

Between the middle and the outer ramparts is a broad range of sharp pillar stones called a *chevaux-de-frise*. A stone lying by itself might move a geologist's adrenaline, but for most of us a single stone is unnoteworthy, perhaps ever boring. When, though, stones are piled one on another and, as here, given shape as walls or fortresses, they take on another meaning—for me, a dark, moribund reminder of the Toilsome past, of the survival battles of our ancestors.

But if they are shaped into dwellings, they become alive, immediate, and utilitarian. One monograph I read stated conclusively that Dún Aengus would hold two hundred cows, while another said over a thousand.

The stones remind me of jelly beans in a glass jar. How many jelly beans, how many stones?

Each stone is a man's effort in lifting, carrying, and

placing. So many stones, so much lifting. The county is endless, the labor awesome.

In the evening, I went to a pub, which was actually called a bar. It was set into a side room of a cottage and run by a man who seemed to be famous for never smiling and rarely talking. There were perhaps thirty people seated around the room, at the bar and at four tables set in corners. There were no seats left, so I and all who followed after me stood.

Nearly everyone there was a native and spoke Irish. In one corner was a group of young women, aged seventeen or eighteen, who were dressed in such a way that I mistook them for mainland girls, and city girls at that. It was only three years before, I was told, that girls began to frequent bars here. There were no older women. But there were many older men, who were treated with sincere deference by the young men, who bought them drinks and spoke to them kindly, never avoiding or patronizing them as we often do in the United States.

A man began to play the accordion, first reels and then more recent music like "Liverpool Lu," which the girls sang. A man sang a song in Irish that I thought would never end. I noticed one girl who had seemed shy in the first hour become overly loud with song after she had a few glasses of stout. I sang "Johnny, I Hardly Knew Ye," and then the bar closed. It was ten-thirty.

I then met two sisters from the mainland, in their late thirties, who were also guests of Mrs. O'Flaherty. They reminded me of Sean O'Faolain characters in the way they presented themselves as being academic, very polite, but genuinely kind. Picked up by Mrs. O'Flaherty, we got into a van and drove to a *ceili* (pronounced "kay-lee," in modern usage meaning a dance) at the Parish Hall in Kilronan (also called the Island Hall, or Halla Ronáin).

The hall, lighted by its own generator, was filled with islanders, and Irish was spoken everywhere around me. In Synge's time the language was declining, and I had noticed turn-of-the-century headstones inscribed in English on the roadside; but very little English is spoken now, and the contemporary road signs and headstones are only in Irish.

There was a drummer and an accordionist on stage, and they announced each dance in Irish. I sat on the side of the hall and watched as the islanders, old and young alike, arranged themselves for a set dance. The music began, and a few of the younger men began to swing their partners madly, creating total disharmony in the set. But nobody seemed to care much, and all seemed to enjoy being knocked about by each other.

It could have been a dance in a suburb of, say, Sacramento, but with different music. There was no traditional dress to be seen—no strange cowhide footwear called "pampooties," no flannel shirts, no black shawls. The men were in flared pants, checked or striped, and knit shirts. Some girls were in blue jeans or long dresses, but many were in short, loose dresses that flew high up as they turned, exposing their underwear. But the men paid no heed at all to this, though I thought it would have been titillating or shameful to the American Irish.

On the mainland of Ireland I had found the men to be generally more good-looking than the women, but here they were equally handsome, and equally spirited, too. The hall was bursting with energy and reckless dancing and spinning. Even the youngest, the eleven- and twelve-year-olds, would not yield the right of way to the older and wilder seventeen- and eighteen-year-olds. All of them, boys and girls alike, braced their shoulders and danced directly into any gyrating couple that happened into their paths.

The Siege of Venice and the Stack of Barley were played, two dances that I knew, and although I felt the will to ask a girl to join me, my regard for my physical safety dissuaded me. I found myself grimacing in anxious expectation as the couples rammed into one another. I would rather be in a fire, I thought, than to dance in my moccasins on that floor.

From a corner of my eye I saw Mrs. O'Flaherty swinging with three others, their hands joined around their backs. Suddenly that group was bounded into and the foursome fell to the floor. I was very concerned for my hostess, but she seemed to care not at all; however, they did sit down after that. I decided then to have one dance for the evening, and Mrs. O'Flaherty and I did a Stack of Barley.

I have never before seen people enjoy themselves with such innocent abandon, and as "The Soldiers' Song," the Irish national anthem, was played at the end of the *ceili*, the men and women held hands or stood with their arms around one another.

We arrived back at the house at two in the morning, and I met the other house guests, a priest from Galway and his niece Colette. We sat beneath a gaslight lamp in the small living room, the only artificial light in the house except for candles. I was wearing an Aran sweater which was remarked on, and over tea Mrs. O'Flaherty told this story:

"It was about tirty years ago—there were only three women on this island that could knit those sweaters, and my mother was one 'a them. Then one day she took sick, and I decided then to learn to do the job myself. And I did learn to do it, and I used to knit sweaters for the men here whose wimen didn't know know to do it themselves. Then we got together, and kind of taught each other how to do it. You know. And there was a man from Dublin used to come here by the name of Farrell, and he used to pay us to make those sweaters. Then he got one woman to copy out the stitches on a piece of paper, and now all the world knows how to do it, and they call them Aran sweaters whether they are made here or no."

"Ahh," said the priest, "if only they could have patented the name of Aran."

As the woman of the house served tea and bread and butter, the conversation was about books and about the film *Man of Aran*. Mrs. O'Flaherty told me that Maggie Dirrane, the woman who was featured in the film, was during her youth her next-door neighbor and that she is still living just a mile or so north of here. I would try to meet her. Mrs. O'Flaherty had seen the film, and I asked her opinion of it.

"I thought good of it," she said, "up until the part where he grabbed her by the hair. Do you remember? Well, if that was his own woman, his own wife, he would not have grabbed her so rough, and I didn't like that at all."

I remembered that the film's featured man and woman were not married, but brought together by Flaherty for the parts. Still, it is an honest documentary of life on the Aran Islands as it was.

Mrs. O'Flaherty, who is vaguely related to the writer Liam O'Flaherty, who was born on Inishmore, was a natural storyteller, although she did not think of herself as one. She didn't flower her words, she got right to the point, and, like many Irish people I've met, she could earn a living as a writer if the opportunity came.

My first day on the Aran Islands closed as I sat on the edge of a huge bed in a small room, hunched over a night table pulled out from the wall. The table and the tablet I was writing on were illumined by soft, wavering candlelight, and beyond the room's solitary window I could hear the Atlantic waters crashing against the rocks—the inescapable, uncontrollable sound of Aran.

I wrote for a while, until my eyes tired from the erratic light. Finally, I lay back on the bed, drew the heavy quilts over me, and tried to discern the sound of the waves from that of the wind. I could feel the solitude and the peacefulness in the air, the kind of quietude that brings forth thoughts of what is close and meaningful, and as I closed my eyes I formed pictures of my wife, Patricia, and my sons, Brendan, Dennis, and Sean, whom I had left on the Irish mainland to dodge traffic between castles, and of Deirdre and Aislinn, our recently born twins, who had been left at home in New York to learn how to walk. I hugged and kissed each image, wishing they were crowded with me in the lumpy, quilt-laden bed, and then I slept.

The next morning was hard with rain. Colette came into the house from the outdoors, the wet dripping from her clothes, her pants rolled up, her shoes in her hands. She said, laughing as she spoke, that she had been walking along in the surf when she came unexpectedly to a ridge and fell down into the ocean. Mrs. O'Flaherty's husband, to whom I had not been introduced and who said very little, asked Colette in Irish if she were retarded, adding that the day was wet enough without going into the sea. They all laughed, and when the remark was translated for me, I laughed too.

In the afternoon, when the rain had subsided, I took a walk about a mile down the road, across a soft beach, and onto a rock shelf, that formed a natural inlet. I sat for a while on folded limestone—folded directly toward the sky—and the wave crests that splashed against the rocks were carried by the wind onto me.

From this place there is a clear view of the white sand of Kilmurvey beach on Inishmore and, across the inlet, of the thatched cottages built by Flaherty for his film. They were two whitewashed huts, one adjoining the other and unlike any cottages I'd seen. I suppose the second cottage was built to give him room to manipulate his camera equipment.

The sun was bright enough to bleach the limestone, and looking across the reflecting sea I could see Gorumna Island off the coast of Connemara.

The climate is more consistently mild on the Aran Islands than on the mainland, the literature and Flaherty's film notwithstanding. There is a saying in Connemara that if you look across the water and you can see the Aran Islands, then it is going to rain, but if you cannot see the islands, then it is already raining.

I sat on the rock and whiled away much of the afternoon, engraving the moments of solitude within me—moments occasionally interrupted by the affronting sounds of a passing motorcycle. There were then over ninety automobiles and two hundred scooters and motorcycles on Inishmore, and it seemed that most of the islanders drove as they danced. The roads are barely wide enough for two compact cars and there are many blind corners. There have been more than a few nonfatal accidents, but unless the government creates a road-improvement program and builds sidewalks for the pedestrians, the convenience of motoring will bring tragedy to Inishmore as surely as the wind sweeps the ancient ruins.

This place, this stone shelf, was idyllic, and the mind could wander effortlessly there. Having spent most of my life in midtown Manhattan, I never discovered empty earth corners, shady glens, or worn haylofts in which to sit quietly and to dream. This place would do. It was as far from the world as I could ever get.

Americans, it seems to me, are the most recent and probably the last tribe of adventurers. There is inherent in our collective personality a lingering pioneer spirit; we have met the sea of the West, but still we are restless. There can be in the United States few more ventures into a virgin wilderness, few more sorties against the unknown strengths of mountains. We have reached a continent's edge and built upward in cloud-tickling towers of commerce. There is nowhere else to go, no new Walden Ponds to measure, no new Manifest Destiny. We have been diminished in spirit to the status of protectors, for we have become burdened with possessions.

On Inishmore, on those folds of ancient limestone, I could lament the passing of the resourceful American adventurer. Yet I could also sense in myself the spirit of the pioneer. Like Natty Bumppo, who kept one step ahead of an everencroaching civilization, I felt that coming here to the Aran Islands was like taking one step out of it. Restlessness ebbed here, for the only civilizing thing around me was a proud history; there were none of the pressures of commerce that we call "civilization" in the United States. But I also felt that I came here not a moment too soon, for the attraction for tourists was building and things were changing.

Distances look greater than they actually are on the Aran Islands, and the walk to Dún Aengus was much less formidable than I had thought. I saw a young girl on the rock-studded path to the hillcrest. She was carrying a book and skipped by me with the lightness of a warming breeze. Would she read the afternoon away, I wondered, in the shadow of the old fortress? Or would she simply look out to the end of the rough ocean and see puff-dreams of Pocahontas, or Maid Marian, or Juliet? Or, perhaps, would she see Cuchulain beating back the sea with his fists?

How the imagination of youth must work in this isolation! But the colors of the mind's vision would soon change like leaves in an autumn wood, for an electric generating station was being built on Inishmore. With television would come the mindless entertainments imported from England or the United States, and the imagination of the Aran people, as manifested in Mrs. O'Flaherty's singing phrases and so notable in Synge's writings, would be in danger of withering away like winter leaves.

The electricity, though, would bring hot water, lighting, and refrigeration to ease the work of a woman like Mrs. O'Flaherty and give her perhaps some idle time to dream on the rocks as she did as a child.

Continuing the climb to Dún Aengus I passed three young women in their early twenties coming down from the fort and chatting casually in Irish. They were probably students here on holiday, but they could have been islanders as well, for it is hard to tell the difference among Irish-speakers. The language, at least for me, seems the only factor distinguishing visitors from islanders, particularly among young women, for there are no island peculiarities in dress or custom as in Synge's time. Synge often referred to pretty girls in petticoats and shifts—in veiled tones of sexuality. When he refers to girls raising their shifts in the ocean, exposing the curves of their legs, the reader feels the artist was constrained in his passion. The freedom of today in manifesting sexual passion, in life or in writing, would probably have thrown Synge for a loss, and he would have been truly shocked watching these women pass by, with their firm young breasts clearly outlined and unharnessed beneath their cotton t-shirts.

Upon reaching the *chevaux-de-frise* that rims the middle rampart of the *dún* (which means "fort"), I decided to leave the pathway and climb over the *abatis* of jagged pillars. The stones, many over six feet in height, are so angled that one could not survive a tripping unscathed, and a thrown rock from the fort hitting its mark here would have done double damage. It took me over five minutes of careful maneuvering to reach the middle rampart itself, and I could only wonder what blood must have stained those stones in battle.

The fort is U-shaped, and the open end of the small inner rampart abuts the three-hundred-foot cliff overlooking the sea. Sitting on the cliff edge, as the child in Flaherty's film did while fishing, I was surprised to feel my stomach turning within me. In my usual work, as a firefighter, I seem to have spent a lifetime on high ladders, and I have often straddled a rung eighty feet above the hard concrete sidewalks of New York. But I was uncomfortable here, the experience touching a natural phobia that I thought I had conquered long ago. Below, far below, was an altar of stone being washed by the waves, and I thought, curiously, in the language of a Synge character, "If I fall from this place it will not be for a swim that I'll be going surely, but I would be breaking my own head open on them stones there."

When Sir William Wilde, a prominent Irish eye and ear surgeon and amateur archaeologist (and father of the playwright Oscar Wilde), visited this very spot in 1857, he lectured a group of visitors from the Ethnological Section of the British Association:

Now why have I brought you here, and more particularly to the spot where I stand at this moment to address you? It is because, after all you have seen, I believe I now point to the stronghold prepared as the last standing place of the Firbolg Aborigines of Ireland, to fight their last battle if driven to the western surge, or as I have already pointed out to you, to take a fearful and eternal departure from the rocks they had contested foot by foot.

Although there was major restoration work done here in the 1890s, there have been no scientific excavations as yet. Consequently, it is pure speculation to date this wondrous fortification, certainly one of the most important antiquities in all of Europe. Even the name "Dún Aengus" is based on speculation. Up until 1839 the fort was called "Dún Mor" (Big Fort). In that year, though, a new ordinance map was made by John O'Donovan, who was told by an old man named Wiggins, himself a descendant of a Cromwellian soldier, that the fort's name was "Dún Innees." O'Donovan took this to mean "Dún Aengus" and so inscribed the fort on the map, though there is no evidence that the fort played a part in the mediaeval literary legend of Aengus Og, a fifth-century chief of the Fir Bolg tribe and the first Christian king of Munster. Adding emphasis to the tenuous nature of island history, the name "Aran" itself seems to have no satisfactory etymology. As translated directly from the Irish, *aran* means bread, which does not seem relevant, but *aru* or *ara*, which means "kidney," is spelled in the genitive as *arann*. With a little imagination, one can see the shape of a kidney in the shape of Inishmore.

I decided to return by walking along the cliffside for a while, passing first a magnificent hole cut out of the rock of a lower ledge. Because of fissuring, a huge and almost perfect rectangle of limestone had dropped into the Atlantic from the ledge, leaving an abyss which at high tide fills with sea water, making of it an Olympic-size swimming pool. It is called "The Worm Hole" be-

10

cause of an island myth that says it is inhabited by a sea serpent.

Moving on, I then came to a great limestone field, an extension, it is said, of the amazing rock fields of the Burren in Country Clare. Within the cracks of this geological wonder are found enough species of flowers to stir the interest of the most hardened botanist—orchids and hoary rockroses and heath bedstraw growing within inches of each other.

Here I met a man named Gregory Connelly, who was sitting on a natural stone seat, resting from a long walk he had taken with his son and five daughters. The children were all young, and he would occasionally call out warnings to them in Irish. Speaking of his oldest, an eleven-year-old boy, he said, "I suppose I did dangerous things on these rocks when I was his age, but I worry for him now." Some of the rock ledges fall ten and fifteen feet, and I shared his concern for the children.

An Inishmore fisherman, Mr. Connelly was in a rough sea some years before and caught his foot in a trawling line that was being let out. The line pulled him into the water, and it was only the strength of his great arms as he clung to the line that kept him from being drowned. His foot was almost severed as he was pulled into the boat, and it was finally amputated some hours after in a Galway hospital.

We spoke of the proper pronunciation of his name, which is "Con*ee*lly," and I was reminded that the Irish in the United States might think of themselves as "Keltic,"

yet at the same time root for the Boston "Seltics."

A highly literate man, he then referred me to an American writer of sea stories named James Brendan Connolly, pronounced more or less as it is spelled, and we laughed over that.

We discussed the economy of Inishmore, which cannot be sustained by the income from a ten-week tourist season. Traditionally, the men of the Aran Islands earned their livelihood by distributing their time between agriculture and fishing, depending on the season, but for those families which have opened their homes to the tourist trade, the man of the house, the classical patriarch, is quickly becoming an adjunct of the woman—feeding the fire, running errands, tending the vegetable garden. The woman who runs the food and lodging business becomes the keystone of the family economy.

If the Aran Islands are to survive economically, Mr. Connelly told me, the fishing industry must be encouraged and protected. Young men will have to be convinced that a good income can be obtained from fishing, reliable enough for them to plan a secure future. One obstacle to this is the current twelve-mile limit that hardly protects Irish fishermen. "Until we get a fifty-mile limit," he said, "we cannot be sure of the fishing industry here on the Aran Islands."

Mr. Connelly owned three fishing boats, and as I looked at the faces of his daughters, among the most beautiful I have ever seen, I wondered if the times would bring them to be sea captains. He then left me and walked with his children toward his village, Gort na gCapall, which is where the writer Liam O'Flaherty was born.

I stayed for a while, watching the ocean dance. The sea becomes like the air on the Aran Islands, part of every second, part of every breath.

In the evening the house was empty but for me and Mrs. O'Flaherty. I asked her if keening, a unique ritual of wailing over the dead, were still done on the Aran Islands. This is what she said:

"No, and isn't it a shame, for I liked it very much, for the women had such beautiful voices. When I was a girl and they began to stop the keening, I thought they didn't respect their dead no more. I did like it very much, the voices in the Irish prayers were so beautiful. The priests didn't like it and made them stop it. It was about twelve or thirteen years ago I was in the grave-yard in Kilronan, and there was an old lady there and she did it, but the priest said something to her and she stopped it. That was the last time I heard it."

I then told her a story I heard in Dublin about how Synge, in his demand for authenticity, needed a keener so that an actress for *Riders to the Sea* could learn the proper method. He found a woman from the Aran Islands living in Dublin, and he and the actress went to her house. The woman tried to keen, but couldn't effectively do it and asked Synge to lie in the bed, close his eyes, and pretend that he was dead. Thereupon she began to keen, with much moving and chanting and clapping of hands, over the famous playwright.

Mrs. O'Flaherty seemed to enjoy that, but made no comment.

The priests, of course, were not so much against keening as they were against the wakes held in the homes, for these wakes where the keening was done were occasions for much drunkenness.

I heard strange sounds while shaving the following morning. The romantic side of me wished they were incantations from beneath the Celtic ground, but upon walking down the stairs I found Father Pat (whose name is Patrick Lynch) saying mass at the sitting-room table, all the occupants of the house save me on their knees before him. There were also a couple of neighbor women, very old but on their knees like the rest, and I saw about one of them the heavy black shawl that had once been so traditional on the Aran Islands. It was the first I'd seen since my arrival. The women now wear sweaters or coats, as on the mainland.

It was raining. At breakfast Mrs. O'Flaherty remembered that she had blessed candles in the house and apologized to the priest for not giving them to him for the mass. "Sure, Mommy," he said in return, "the light of faith is all we need for the mass."

My morning was spent reading and talking. I also walked again to the rock folds by the beach at the Kilmurvey inlet. The rain was light and soon gave way to the sun. This little rock shelf was convenient, just a twenty-minute walk from the house, and represented to me all of what Inishmore was—aged, beaten, alone. It offered protection from the incessant swells. It brought the kind of separation from the world that gives rise to a pilgrimage of imagination.

Father Pat and Colette were leaving by air after lunch (called "dinner" here), and Mrs. O'Flaherty and I decided to go along for the ride to Killeany, where the small, eight-passenger plane landed. It was just a short strip of grassy ground where the grazing horses were driven away just seconds before the plane touched down.

There was an hour to pass before the plane landed, and we went to the American Bar to have a parting drink. The place was named for an islander that had been to the United States, saved from money he earned, and returned to open the business. I noticed many young islanders drinking there, some of them already drunk, and was told that there is no other diversion for them when the meager work on their small farms is done.

I thought of Gregory Connelly and of how much better off these young men would have been if they were out fishing. I also remembered drinking beer at their age, and although I am always sad when I see young men drinking beyond their capacity, the possible sanctimoniousness of my sadness does not escape me.

We said good-bye to the priest and Colette, and then I went to Kilronan to rent a bicycle. I am not inherently lazy, but I find walking as a utilitarian form of transportation to be disconcerting. I would prefer a car or motorcycle to get from point A to point B, but a bicycle would at least seem to shorten the distance. I like to walk very much, but only after I have determined in my mind to "go for a walk." Henceforth on this island I would only walk from the point Bs.

At the high tea, which is like our supper, I met new residents, a teacher from Drogheda, in County Louth, on the northeast coast of the mainland, and a couple from Cork, on the southeast, who had been here before. The teacher had a very low opinion of the United States, and among his views was the dictum that success in that country could only come with dishonesty and corruption. I gave him a short lesson in American history in an attempt to disabuse him of his prejudices, but there can be no shadows in a young idealist's mind, and it is not surprising that they oftentimes become sun-blinded.

In the evening, Mrs. O'Flaherty and I talked about the Irish language, how it declined during Synge's time, and then again came to be the first language of the Arans. One of the reasons English was used here was because the islanders were looked down upon by the people of Galway, so they learned English to diminish the differences between them and the mainland people. This, remember, was when Ireland was part of Great Britain. After Ireland's independence, though, the Irish language again flourished in the islands. Mrs. O'Flaherty told me this story:

"When I was a young girl I had to go to hospital in Galway. Now the Galway people didn't like the people from the Aran Islands. They thought we were uncivilized, do you know what I mean, and the nurses there treated me meanly. They didn't do anything for me, because when I went there I said to myself that I would use my own language there, and I spoke only Irish. But then on the last day, the day I was leaving, I picked up a book and read to them in English. Now, I read to them in English, and they didn't like that at all."

Afterward, Mrs. O'Flaherty's son, Máirtin (who was called "Maucheen"), came and we had a talk. He had acted in the Irish theater in Galway and also had a play he had written in Irish produced. He said that he liked to write, but liked the jar more. He was only twenty, though looked and talked as if he were older. Premature aging, I thought, can come equally to a man who drinks too much and to one suffering the internal turmoil of a budding writer. Máirtin thought he liked to drink, as I suspect many young writers I have known like to drink, in a soft emulation of a hard Hemingway.

"If there were a row of naked women on the floor," he related, "with a jar at the end, I would walk over them. It's less complicated."

Máirtin persuaded me to a walk to the pub, and on the way he taught me a few Irish phrases of congeniality. There we joined other islanders. Máirtin did not introduce me to any of his friends—introductions did not seem to be the custom here. They spoke in Irish though they realized I did not know the language, and only one of a crowd of twelve or so went out of his way to speak to me and only then to ask me about a song I had sung two nights before. One cannot say the Inishmore people are friendly, and it seems to me that they care little for people who do not speak their tongue. I felt as Mrs. O'Flaherty must have felt in the Galway hospital, although she was able to see the irony of being bilingual. It all seemed to me a sad reversal to her story—the young Aran Islanders appeared xenophobic. But, then, the Irish have always been an internal people, not very concerned with the world about them. I have heard that said in relation to the decline of art and monasticism in Ireland in the thirteenth century. The classical world of the Mediterranean passed them by.

Later in the evening I went to another *ceili* at the Island Hall, this less crowded and therefore less wild than Sunday's. I wore shoes instead of moccasins and determined to have a dance. Máirtin was there and suggested I ask a certain girl to do a Siege of Venice. The girl smiled at first but went sour when she found out I was American. I managed the dance with little pleasure. Next I asked a girl who turned out to be a visitor from Cork to join me in a Stack of Barley. She didn't know how to do it, and I did my best to teach her, reconstructing the steps from the memories of a hundred Bronx wedding receptions.

After forty-five minutes or so, the island priest, a red-faced, overfed man, came into the Island Hall and nodded to the accordion player. In the middle of a wild set dance, the music changed suddenly and the dancers came to attention for "The Soldiers' Song," the national anthem. Although I was disappointed, for I thought it must have been the shortest *ceili* in the history of Ireland, the dancers didn't seem at all distressed as they filed out of the hall. "He's just showing his authority," a young man said to me, referring to the priest.

The following day was wet and cold, delighting me. I breakfasted first, said good-bye to Mr. and Mrs. O'Flaherty, promising that I would return within the week, and bicycled through the rain to Kilronan and the M.S. *Naomh Eanna*. I was going to Inishmaan, and I felt as the ship drifted from the pier that I was leaving the nineteenth century behind in Inishmore and traveling to the eighteenth.

Synge's Aran Islands journal opens on Inishmore, but after just nine pages it changes abruptly to Inishmaan where nearly all of the rest of the book takes place. Few tourists go to the Middle Island and therefore, I thought, it would probably be unaffected by the tourist trade—souvenir shops, colorful carts, and all the hawking that goes with them. Not that Inishmore could in any way be considered a Coney Island. Still, because of its busyness, its flow of tourists, and a harbor that permits ships' entry, then as now, the natural simplicity of life that Synge was searching for could still be found only in the remotest parts, like the rock steps near the beach or the limestone fields near Dún Aengus.

The ship anchored about two hundred yards from shore, the curraghs already fighting the tumbling waters toward it. Five of these canvas, lath, tar-covered, thin-spined vessels, so ancient in their design, arrived at the side of the ship. I descended into the hold and stood across from a large door built into the bulkhead. Soon I was told to take the curragh that was bringing the mail; it was pointed out to me by a seaman. There were, besides the mail and two rowers, thirty heavy gas cylinders piled high in the curragh, going to Galway for refilling. One man held the small craft against the ship while the other lifted the cylinders from it, his task made heavier by the constant rising and lowering of the sea, and his formidable fists banging steadily against the ship. The mail bag was lifted to the *Naomh Eanna* and I began to get ready for my descent into the curragh, but a seaman held me back saying, "Not yet, lad, there's time," proceeding then to lift eighty-pound bags of fertilizer and almost throwing them to the curragh. An old woman stood quietly in the back of the hold waiting for the seaman to give her a nod. It was an old ritual for her, I thought. Twelve bags later I was told to climb down and sit on one of the bags. It was hard rain and jumping waters the whole of the short trip to shore, and

I was greatly excited. There is a childish thrill in riding this strange vessel, and it brought memories of Saturday nights in Playland of Rockaway Beach. The curragh sides were occasionally level with the sea, and there was much splashing through the cold air, yet it wasn't as wild as I had hoped. The curragh, when controlled by these island men, can actually climb over the highest of waves, and I found myself wishing for a sudden storm, a kind of existential binge. I said nothing as the rowers pulled against the sea, nor did they, but one smiled at me, I guess upon seeing the excitement in my eyes. These were fierce-looking men, in their twenties, with long curly hair and small tragic eyes embroidering their rawhide faces, and I got the feeling that the smile was a rare gift.

I was told to go to the post office two miles up the only island road. There were no cars on this island, or even horsetraps, and I began to walk. I soon overtook two little girls who had come to watch the boat come in, and were returning to their homes. They were speaking Irish, which is, of course, the first language of the islands. The school children are taught English here as a mandatory second language, just as Irish is taught as a mandatory second language in the schools throughout Ireland.

I talked to them through the rain and wind while walking the sand and gravel road. One didn't understand me very well, a redheaded and red-faced spark named Theresa Flaherty, and I felt insecure repeating myself to the child, although it seemed fun to her. The other, named Mary Kearney, the Galway-raised sister of the island curate, more easily understood my American accent. They pointed out the local bar, shop, and post office, all of which are in private houses made public at convenience. They left me at a blue-shuttered house, and I walked further to the post office. A woman there, who had one of the two phones on the island, apologized for not having the room she had promised me and directed me back to the blue-shuttered house where she had arranged for me to stay.

Inside I met the Mulkerrinses, who owned the house. The woman was a warm-faced but taciturn person, and so very unlike Mrs. O'Flaherty of Inishmore. The man seemed much older than the woman and, I later learned, spoke little English. Considerately, the woman gave me a towel to dry myself, made me tea, and showed me to a recently built and comfortably arranged room.

I returned to the cement-floored sitting room, and watched the old man break small pieces of wood for the coal stove. A young man and an older woman were also sitting. They spoke Irish and never looked in my direction. I felt like an ornament or a dusty picture—quite incidental. After a disconcerting length of time I said, "The little girl told me she was a Kearney. I am related to the Kearneys. They are from Kilkenny."

The young man looked over and told me kindly, almost sympathetically, that he was also a Kearney, from

Galway, and that he was the island priest. I was relieved, and the talk progressed in interest from there. It is their way to be restrained among strangers.

The priest, who wore no collar most of the time, had lived in the house for about a year, ever since he volunteered for the assignment after ordination. He didn't seem more than twenty-five or so and spent most of the time building a residence with his own hands and occasional help from the parishioners, across the road and next to the church.

I asked about Synge's stay on this island, and Father Kearney told me that the writer had lived just three houses away and that the house was still in the same family.

At dinner I met the other residents of the house, three Irish Christian Brothers, all named John. They had come to Inishmaan to speak their language, one of them evidently having been there many times. They were all teachers and supporters of the Irish language, and a debate occurred on the future of it.

There are five or six *Gaeltacht* (Irish-speaking) areas in the entire country, and only fifty thousand native Irish-speakers. But there are another fifty thousand enthusiasts, like the brothers, who have learned Irish as a second language and speak it as much as they can, preferring it to English. Besides the Aran Islands, there are *Gaeltacht*s in Connemara in Galway, southwest Kerry, Donegal, Waterford, and Meath.

One of the brothers predicted that the language would be dead in thirty or so years and illustrated the argument by naming many small villages where the language is declining. The others vociferously argued by naming more villages to which the language has spread. The first brother answered, "I would love it if what you say is true, but I cannot believe it is." The word "love" I found appropriate, for that was another way of defining their enthusiasm for the language. They had traveled to Inishmaan, after all, because it was said to be the place where the purist Irish was spoken. I was told that there are ways of saying things in Irish, particularly humorous ambiguities, that cannot be done in English, but then that is probably true the other way around. The Irish language, I think, ought to be encouraged though, if only to instill and reinforce a sense of nationalism in the people.

The daily mass was held in the evening here, and after dinner, and following a small, predetermined walk, I went to the church, which was about fifty yards from where I was living. Built in 1939, it stands near the site of a fifteenth-century church that was razed in the name of our Lord and progress. I would have preferred, I think the older church to the new one. It is, of course, a small church, with worn, wood flooring and an interesting parquet ceiling above bare rafters. I knelt a moment on the hard wood kneeler and sat on the bench watching the people arrive. I fortunately sat on the right side of the center aisle, for as the women came in they sat on the left and the men on the right. This without exception. About twenty each of men and women came. The men wore heavy work clothes, their small visored caps in their hands. The women wore coats, except for the older women, who still wore the traditional long red skirts and colorful knitted shawls which they wrap around their shoulders and tie at the lower back. It is a simple and beautiful outfit. Father Kearney said the mass in the vernacular—Irish—and it reminded me of the historical continuity of the old Latin mass I knew as a child and teenager. Understanding neither the Latin nor the Irish version brought to me a strange and paradoxical sense of security in the religion as it was taught to me. That is, that faith always transcends understanding.

In the evening, a young student named Cormac and I went together to the bar lounge. He was seventeen and wanted to be a writer. He liked American literature, particularly the stories of J. D. Salinger and the poetry of Carl Sandburg, and asked if I would make him a reading list.

Women did not frequent the bar on Inishmaan, but they did go into the attached lounge, and only since it opened several years ago. Not more than twenty people came in, about half of them visitors. The Christian Brothers were there, and another small group of men who were also brothers. The islanders here did not seem to drink as much as on Inishmore, and the young men in the lounge were very quiet. Many songs were sung in Irish, only one in English, and a beautiful girl played the tin whistle. With this girl was another even more beautiful girl, a vision of Cathleen Ni Houlahan, with small brown eyes that nervously scanned the room. They were sisters, I was told.

The visitors and islanders were known to each other and seemed truly to thrive on the bantering that went on between songs in the hour or so we spent in the lounge. I wondered if it was the Irish language that facilitated the gaiety of the conversations or the fact that all the visitors, except Cormac and me, were members of a religious order (the Irish being particularly considerate of the clergy). Again, there were no introductions, and I felt constrained to weave my English into the charming pattern of their language. I was content to listen. Yet, I think it is fair to say, I felt a slowly emerging embarrassment that came from my ignorance of the language. I found that I was beginning to regret that I could not speak Irish, though it was less a distress than a kind of existentialist yearning.

While walking back through the dark and breeze, Cormac played "Carolan's Concerto" on a tin whistle he had borrowed, and the sound echoed from the thousand silver walls. It is my favorite tune.

Thick smoke in a small room is not as dark as cloud-covered Inishmaan at night, and although Cormac walked steadily enough, I had to stop several times to feel my way along the rock walls that rim the road. The dark will change eventually, though, for electricity is planned for this island also. Walking home, at one with the black night and faraway glimmering stars, will be but a memory for these islanders, I thought.

Progress will come inevitably. Development houses will be built on these age-weary shores, telephone poles will rise like modern totem poles, and automobiles will grind along the rocky roads that were meant for pampooties. Still, the Aran Islands will maintain their great appeal of isolation, the rain will still fall as the wind rises, and it will still be a long way to the mainland. The peace that is Aran's will be preserved by the cruel, whipping, bridge-less sea.

After shaving the next morning I waited in the front room until breakfast was ready. It was the room that the front door opened into, where visitors were received, and where the old man sat with his ear to the radio. There were two tables, each bordered by two chairs, and a coal stove that also had two chairs, one on either side of it. At the far wall stood a glossy, painted hutch over-filled with dishes and cups and saucers. The walls were painted the same indigo blue as the outside shutters. Many religious pictures, papal blessings, calendars, and prayers—each ornate and colorful—hung on the walls, softening the effect of the gray concrete floor. The ceiling was made of yellow wood slats. I cannot remember ever seeing a room like it in the United States.

Above the coal stove was a dark oil painting of an old Aran woman made by the Irish artist Sean Keating on one of his visits here. I would guess it was of no small value, for the artist is of good reputation in Ireland.

The subject of the painting both smiled and frowned. He saw the Aran character—the edge of despair—and the Aran heart—the simple merriment—and brought them together. It is a painting I would like to own, not for its value, but for its lesson.

A bruised chicken, nursed back to health by Mrs. Mulkerrins, shared the room with me.

After breakfast I walked to the end of the island, saying hello to all who passed on the road—four or five people. As I passed the houses, the people were busy painting, sawing, feeding the chickens that seemed to be everywhere, or hand-reaping and tying the grass. More than half the houses on Inishmaan are still thatched, although they are not thatched around the chimneys anymore. Many of the houses—there are not more than sixty all together—were built within the last forty or fifty years, like the one I am living in, and have roofs of slate or tile. There are even three modern ranch houses with picture windows. Almost all of the houses are built on a hill in the middle of the island, about a mile and a half from the sea on either side of the road. I understood for the first time today the need of a horse in Synge's play *Riders to the Sea,* for it is a rugged distance to the pier for the fishermen to walk, though I saw only two horses on the island while I was there. I was told that the horses were taken to the mainland for the summer grazing.

I walked about a mile to the west end of the island. One cannot hide from the beautiful views that are pervasive here, and I several times nearly walked into walls because of them.

I came to a museum that was founded just a year before by a woman from Galway. It was a traditional thatched house on the north side of the road, near the road's end, the highest building on Inishmaan. The hearth and the cooking and fishing implements hung around it are just as they were in Synge's time and before. I bought a small print of boys, dressed in long petticoats, sitting on a wall. The age-old custom of dressing all preadolescent boys in girls' clothes to confuse the boy-snatching fairies was abandoned forty or so years ago.

It was told to me that at one time, much before Synge, the boys wore dresses until their twentieth birthday, and it is a plausible bit of information when the idea of an isolated culture is considered. But from the middle of the nineteenth century, philologists of all kinds began to visit the Aran Islands, and the custom, perhaps when viewed by outsiders, embarrassed the older boys. The wearing of petticoats by younger boys, and I supposed the belief in evil fairies, persisted for more than twenty years after Synge's death in 1909. Mrs. O'Flaherty on Inishmore remembered seeing boys in petticoats when she was a child.

I walked to the end of the road, which had become just broken rock, climbed over a wall, and went on to the west end of the island. It was near here that Synge dreamed and wrote on a rock formation they now call Synge's Chair. I sat nearby on a cluster of rocks, entranced by the world before me—the multiblues of the Atlantic straight to the west, the rock cliffs of Inishmore to the north, the waves being forced into crevices there and soaring forty and fifty feet into the air. Just a few feet from me were sheep pecking at the bits of grass that grow in the thin spaces between the rocks. They were gentle and occasionally looked my way questioningly. The air, cold as November, went through my windbreaker, but I sat for an hour or so in determined reverence. I would have sat longer, but I watched a dark cloud come in from the Atlantic, and I was halfway to the Mulkerrins house when the rain started to bounce from the ground. I stood against a high stone wall for a while, and when the cloud passed I continued on my way.

There was a man in the rear of the house where Synge lived, and he called out to me in Irish. I told him I had no Irish, and he asked where in America I came from, continuing quickly that he had been in Boston. He then named, for my edification, the towns surrounding Boston, pleased with his knowledge and that he was able to share it.

"Is this the house Synge lived in?" I asked, quite sure that it was. After his nod, I said, "Then you must be Mr. Faherty." And we talked over the stone wall.

"You know," he told me, "when Synge was here, nobody paid much mind to him, and he died young, didn't he, and had no chance of coming much here. If he came today, even ten, twenty years ago, people would come from miles around to see him."

I asked about Michael, the young boy of this household who had been Synge's island guide and Irish tutor. "He died around nineteen-fifty-eight or fifty-nine," I was told. "But the baby that was in this house still lives on the island. He's seventy-four or six." I remembered the sick child in Synge's book *The Aran Islands,* and when its mother made a trip to Galway, a wet nurse had to be found for it. I asked who the man and woman of the house were when Synge lived there and was told, "That would be my wife's father's father and mother, Mike MacDonagh and his wife Bridg." He then told me his name, Mike Faherty, and that he liked Americans. Another cloud began to pass, and it rained as before, flooding off the rock between us. It appeared that he was willing to continue the talk in the downpour, but I thought he was just being polite. I introduced myself in parting, and he invited me to come to the house the following day.

In the evening I taught Father Kearney a few chords on an old guitar and then walked down to the bar lounge.

There were thirty-one people in the lounge that night—we five from Mrs. Mulkerrins' house were the only visitors and the rest were natives. As in the church, the men and women were seated on different sides of the room, except for two married couples. There was no dating here, and the young could get together only at a *ceili*, which was irregularly scheduled in winter and weekly in summer. I had not seen a young man and a young woman together since my arrival. The young women, who were watched over very carefully by their families and friends, all left together at midnight, just an hour and a half after their arrival.

Music is not a strong tradition here as it is in other *Gaeltacht* areas, but a few islanders could always be prodded to offer a song or two. When they sang, they stared directly in front of them or looked down because of their natural shyness, and often a friend sitting by their side would hold their hand to support them through the song. That was true of the men as well as women. The gesture was referred to as "pumping the song up."

There was a young man who played the accordion, and one of the Christian Brothers danced a reel. The young man, though, played only three or four tunes on his instrument, and even then he had to be encouraged by his friends. The young married woman played a very complicated jig on the tin whistle, to the delight of all except perhaps her husband, who had returned from Galway and seemed to say nothing all night long. Father Kearney told me it would take years to really know these quiet, unique people, and I believe him.

Since I was up half the night writing by candlelight, I woke the next day well past eleven. I breakfasted hurriedly—tea and biscuits—and went to the Faherty house. Mrs. Faherty greeted me warmly, pulled a chair out in front of the coal burner for me, and we talked. She is a mother of eight children, nearing sixty years of age, yet the lineaments of great beauty are still found in her face, and youthful laughter can be seen in the shining, powder-blue eyes.

The north door of the cottage was opened, and we looked out on a religious view of the distant Connemara hills throught the mist. The Faherty family had expanded, and in the backyard a foundation had been built for their new house that would block completely the present view. Mrs. Faherty told me about the visitors, mostly professors and students, who come to "Synge's house," as the Fahertys call it. She showed me how the house was expanded by two rooms since Synge's day. The place was still very small—four or five rooms at most. It was well kept, newly whitewashed, the thatch on the roof maintained, and there was a picturesque cabbage patch and garden in the front yard.

Mrs. Faherty talked of Synge and said pretty much what her husband had said before—that no one paid much attention to Synge while he was here. He would, she said, sit in the corner, next to where we were, and listen to the talk around the hearth. A Connelly cousin of her grandparents had been drowned on a curragh trip about Synge's time, Mrs. Faherty went on. Connelly was taking a pony to the Galway fair when he was thrown from the curragh. At about the same time a boy from Kilronan on Inishmore (which is called "the Big Island" here, never by its name) was washed up on the shores of Donegal, way to the north, after being missing

for two weeks.* Synge evidently combined these two unrelated deaths for *Riders to the Sea.* By the fire, Synge also heard the story of a County Mayo man named Mailly, who, in a row, killed his father and hid out here in this house. From this character, of course, Synge created "Christy Mahon," the "Playboy of the Western World." Mailly finally was caught and taken to Galway but escaped again, to the United States.

I mentioned to Mrs. Faherty that Synge wrote of the MacDonaghs' fascination with his watch and that Synge had promised to send the family a clock. Mrs. Faherty said that she remembered her mother talking about a clock that Synge sent but didn't know what happened to it.

Mr. Faherty then walked in, his cowhide pampooties muddy and squishing, and we sat across from each other. I offered him a cigarette, which he patiently puffed on, although he doesn't smoke, accepting it as a courtesy. He promised to make me a pair of pampooties and took a measurement of my foot. Before parting, I asked Mr. Faherty if this house would be torn down when he and his family were living in the new house.

"Surely," he replied, "they're tearing down enough things, and this cottage is known the world over. So it will stay as it is. For a while, anyway."

Time had passed quickly, and I wanted yet to climb to

*At least, that is what the Fahertys said. Synge's account in *The Aran Islands* has the boy a native of Inishmaan.

the huge pre-Christian fort that was nearby. There is another fort, or *dún*, as they are called here, a mile down the road toward the east. The one near us is called Dún Conor and the other Dún Moher (also known as Dún Farvagh). Mrs. Faherty told me the way to Dún Conor, which, although nearby, is still a healthy walk.

"Synge said it was 'just a stone's throw from the cottage,'" I said, adding with a smile, "Synge must have had a strong arm."

Mrs. Faherty laughed and said, "It is told that there was only one hammer to break the stones on this island in the days when the *dúns* were made. They would work on Dún Moher for half a day and then throw the hammer over to Dún Conor. Now, that is a strong arm that threw that distance."

Dún Conor is called a "round" fort, although it is an oval in shape, the north–south distance from wall to wall being two hundred twenty-seven feet and the east–west distance one hundred fifteen feet. The *dún* is made of small rocks, as are the thousands of walls on the Aran Islands, fitted together without mortar of any kind. It is a monument to man's labor, for the walls are twelve to eighteen feet thick and fifteen to twenty feet high. I thought as I stood on top of the highest part of the wall, the wind and light rain blowing hard, that there one could experience a unique and personal tie with one's Celtic history.

There was an exclusivity about it for me, made possible by its remoteness, by its overwhelming strength, and by the enigmatic designs of the interior rock formations, all of which gave rise to my sense of an internalized Celtic past.

Today's Celts—in Brittany, Ireland, Wales, Scotland, Cornwall, and the Isle of Man—are reaching for their past, reviving their Gaelic languages, reinstating the ambiguous Celtic art forms that bridge the civilizations of East and West, the supernatural and the natural. But while some of the world's Celts seek their identity and press for autonomy, historical continuity seems secure enough here on Inishmaan and assured for the future— "For a while, anyway," as Mr. Faherty might say. Electricity, when it comes, is certain to darken the memories of the past as much as it will brighten the houses of the future.

Related directly to the Battle-ax people of the Neolithic period, the Celts began civilizing Central Europe before Hammurabi brought his code of laws to Babylon in 2000 B.C. In the eighth century B.C., when the blind poet Homer was seeing visions of Odysseus and the legendary founders of Rome, Romulus and Remus, were licking the smooth side of the she-wolf, the Celts were already a distinct and viable group, building, inventing, using iron, and creating order. They dominated Europe for seven centuries, developing handsaws, chisels, files, soap, chain armor, horseshoes, plowshares, and flour mills. They flourished until the rise of Rome and the much later rise of Anglo-Saxon England sent them scurrying to the west—to the fields of Brittany, to the hills of Wales, to the appendicle of Cornwall, to the mountains of Scotland, and across the water to the Isle of Man and the rocks of Ireland. Some ended in the Aran Islands, there to begin the never-ending toil of rock carrying. I sat in utter aloneness for an hour, on the rampart of Dún Conor, a monument to their travels and their labors.

Although Synge's work brims with Celtic allusions, he never directly wrote about the importance of a Celtic past on the Aran Islands. Yet, he must have been interested in the art work of the islands' burial crosses and the architecture of the *dún*s and the old church, for he was an inquiring man. But since Synge had an Anglo-Irish Protestant background that would not be considered true Celtic, I suppose he felt no personal attachment to the history that surrounded him on Inishmaan.

Two grazing cows ambled through the *dún*'s passageway, and I played to them on the bagpipes I had carried with me. I once heard that the definition of an Irish gentleman is one who knows how to play the bagpipes, but does not. Notwithstanding, the cows seemed to enjoy the music as it filled the inner rampart, a dirge that whistled out to sea like a hymn.

After dinner I sat by the coal stove with closed eyes and listened to Mrs. Mulkerrins talk with her daughter Maureen. Though unaware of what was said, I took much pleasure in the ring of the words. Maureen had just turned eighteen and had another year to complete at an Irish-speaking secondary school in Galway. All children here leave the island at fourteen or fifteen for a mainland school in Galway, returning home only on holidays. The expense is covered by government grants, but it seems to be a system that motivates emigration. After this education, almost all the young people leave the island for work in Ireland's cities or in England. Since there is no pier on Inishmaan, the bigger fishing boats cannot be based there and consequently cannot employ the island's young men for either fishing or dock work. The islanders themselves, being without a pier, are also precluded from buying or investing in the more competitive fishing vessels. Although a new sweater-making factory employs ten people, there is little work on Inishmaan besides lobster fishing from curraghs, and for most, income is meager and supplemented by government dole. (This is largely true on the other islands also, although Inishmore at least has an income-producing tourist trade and Inisheer has a transient student population which adds to the economy of that island. The people of all three islands receive government subsidies for speaking Irish.) One cannot get rich on these islands.

The bar lounge was very crowded later that evening, for four young men had returned on holiday from London and all of their friends came to celebrate. I spent only an hour there, but it was filled with singing, many of the songs, I was told, composed by islanders. I was introduced to the tin-whistler's husband, who is in charge of the economic development of the islands. It is, of course, his job to be optimistic about the economic development of Inishmaan, and he spoke about the inevitability of a pier being built here. The island, I thought, would suffer the loss of this remoteness that so attracted me, once a Galway ship was able to dock here; the idea of coming to land without the curragh was truly saddening. On the other hand, Inishmaan belonged to the islanders, not to my or anyone else's romantic notion or to Synge's memory, and a tourist trade would greatly improve the economy here as it had on the big island. However, I would not like to live on Inishmaan when that time came, for the island was not big enough for one to escape the tourists as one could on Inishmore. One would be better situated in a cabin in Vermont seeking solitude, although there would be no kings or saints buried there.

In the morning, Sunday, the colorful everyday crocheted shawls were replaced at mass by the dress shawls which were handwoven of brown and tan wool and embroidered with intricate designs. The rows of old women on the left side of the church looked like a museum exhibition of craftmanship, and I paid more attention to those shawls than to the mass.

Afterward I packed my bag, shook hands with the Mulkerrinses, and walked to the small cement landing, talking only to a horse and a few sheep along the way. The curraghs were overturned on the beach, and I ran my hand over the smooth tar finish. These fourteen-foot craft have almost no resistance, no friction, on the water and that is why they can roll over a mighty wave as ducks ride a ripple. Before World War I, a curragh could be bought for $18.00; in 1970 one cost $75.00; but when I was there seven years later I was told they cost about $400.00.

I sat on a stone and watched the beach area come alive with the islanders, many of them going, as I was, to the curragh races to be held that day on Inisheer, the small East Island. The men picked the curraghs up, crawled beneath them, and carried them to the water, flipping them over as other islanders made ready to step into them. I got into a curragh, and as it moved effortlessly from the landing, I suddenly became aware of the islanders' beautiful faces—strong, determined people all around me, their hair blowing in the wind of history.

I was sad to leave Inishmaan, without knowing why really. The people there, while friendlier than those on Inishmore, were not naturally warm and generous. They were isolates, transfixed within their own language, suspicious of those who did not speak it. Also, an introduction on any of these islands was as rare as limousines. Even in the Mulkerrinses' house, though I sensed this warmth, I did not formally meet either the old man or his daughter, and in their company I felt like Ralph Ellison's "invisible man." Still, Inishmaan was a purgation, the traditional ways and the distance from complex civilization good for the spirit. Only an idiot or a dilettante boulevardier could pass through here without learning more of himself.

Unlike all of the other curraghs in the water, mine was being pushed forward by a small motor hooked onto stern. The curraghman, Sean Faherty, who was about thirty, was wearing dress slacks and a sports shirt. He was a lobster fisherman in the summer, and he earned enough in that endeavor to carry him over the year. I asked if it was possible for the lobsters to be fished out, and he replied, "No, I don't think so. They've been saying that for the last ten years, but they are still here anyway."

Newly married, Sean had no children as yet, but he did own one of the modern, ranch-style houses built on Inishmaan recently. He was the kind of man described to me by Gregory Connelly who represented the future of the Aran Islands. The young men who now save their earnings to buy houses or property used to spend every penny that found its way into their pockets. They are looking toward a future on the Aran Islands and are confident it will come if the fishing holds up.

The small landing on Inisheer was busy with lobster boats and curraghs riding the waves at its side. The natives of Inishmore, Inishmaan, and the town of Doolin in County Clare had come to participate in the Inisheer curragh races, which is actually a series of loosely organized competitions on land as well as sea. As I walked from the landing I saw a curragh coming in from Inishmaan oared by a man and a woman. I'd not seen a woman rowing a curragh before.

I carried my bag just a short distance to the lodging house operated by Mrs. Conneely. It seemed that nearly everyone I'd met on the Aran Islands was named Connelly, Conneely, Gill, McGill, Flaherty, Faherty, O'Flaherty, or Mullins.

Mrs. Conneely, a broad-faced, smiling woman, famous for the Aran sweaters she knits, showed me the way to my room, passing ten or so young girls in the hallway. In their early teens, the girls had come from all parts of Ireland, including Ulster, to study the Irish language at a college that is situated here. Unpacking my bag, I could hear them singing in harmony as they walked down the road. Occasionally, the sound of a gull squawked above them.

There was a crowd gathered on a playing field about a mile from Mrs. Conneely's house. Quite a few of the older men were wearing the traditional black woolen pants and vest and the cowhide pampooties. These slippers are roughly cut to the size of the foot, tied with cord at the front and back, and worn with the hair on the outside. They must be constantly damp or they will dry and shrink, so they are kept in a pail of water during the nights. They are a practical shoe for walking on slippery rocks, for a person's toes can be used as I suppose God meant them to be used; but pampooties are not as handsome or advanced as the American Indian moccasin. All the women wore dresses or slacks, and I saw no traditional shawls, that mode of dress seemingly in favor in only the Middle Island.

In the center of the crowd was a small neutral space, just long enough for a runner to approach the posts and lintel of a high jump. A young man jumped and the crowd sighed in chorus, delighted that the cross bar was not knocked over.

I saw the young woman who had rowed the curragh from the Middle Island and introduced myself. Her name is Gobnait, named after the sixth-century patroness of bees, St. Gobnat, one of Ireland's most revered saints. Gobnait and her husband, not yet thirty years old, are teachers in Drogheda, far to the east on the mainland, but they have built one of the modern houses on Inishmaan where they both were born. "We have the best of both worlds," she told me, meaning that they have stable, well-paid positions on the mainland and can spend all their holidays on the island of their youth. Gobnait was the first woman, she thought, ever to handle the oars of a curragh, and she did that, coincidentally, about the same time the bar lounges on the islands were opened to the female population.

I asked if there were many professional people that came from her island, and she said that while there are a few teachers who were born and raised on Inishmaan, there were no doctors or lawyers that she knew of. A modern woman, Gobnait respresented still another new kind of Aran Islander, who, with newfound affluence and leisure, had determined that her ties to the past and the purity in island life were worth preserving. Unlike so many who had fled these islands before her, she had found a way to nourish her roots while maintaining a position in the larger world.

The crowd then moved like a sea to another place on the field, where a running broad jump was to be held. Afterward, they moved to where the hammer-throw contest was to take place, and again they left little room in the middle for contestants. One man stepped forward to throw the thirty-four-pound hammer, but he lost his stride and the heavy iron went sailing toward the crowd, scattering them. No one, fortunately, was hurt, but there was much ooing and aahing before the throng returned to their original places and revived the danger.

The running broad jump was next, and then the tug of war. The athletes performed enthusiastically and competently, and the sports gave great pleasure to the islanders. There was no betting, and indeed there seems to be no gambling at all on Aran Islands.

Meanwhile, some of the island children had brought their donkeys to the field, and all the children had a great romp on the backs of the animals. One donkey in particular kept bucking the riders off, to everyone's delight.

While most of the people went to the beach to watch the curragh race, I walked to the end of the landing where there was a clearer view of the ocean. The weather had turned foul, and a great biting wind struck through my sweater as I watched the vessels fight the wind and the waves. A man standing by said to me, "The weather like this makes them row faster."

"I have no doubt about that," I answered, "to get them out of it."

The curragh races were held according to the age of the rowers, three rowers to a boat, but the distance, about a circular mile, was the same in all categories. The curraghs moved surprisingly fast over the rough seas, the oars and the backs of the rowers moving with computer precision. The crowd on the strand gave a loud cheer and clapped vigorously as the first winning curragh was beached.

At dinner I was served what looked to be a perfectly cooked club steak, but turned out to be a piece of pot roast fried on both sides. The food on the Aran Islands is bland, as it is in most of Ireland. Like the English, who made a fortune and a colonial empire out of the spice route, yet never leaned to use the stuff they were transporting properly, the Irish, except in a few fine restaurants, seem to have never progressed beyond salt and pepper. On the Aran Islands, fish is seldom served because it is an income product, and I am reminded of the proverbial tailor whose pants need patching.

There were two bars on Inisheer, one near where I was staying and the other in the middle of the island. In the evening I went to the distant one, for it was near the Parish Hall where a *ceili* was to be held. On the road to this bar and scattered all around it were empty beer and soda bottles and paper wrappers of all kinds. The Aran Islands are generally clean and well kept, but there is no one employed on any island to remove the litter from the roadsides. Even isolated spots of disorderliness, though, as on the road to the bar near the Parish Hall, can mar the memory of a joyful journey.

The bar was packed tighter than an American singles bar on a Friday night, everyone busy celebrating the victories of the day and toasting the defeats. I passed the time listening to the music that was coming from a corner of the room. There were a flutist, two accordionists, a man playing the spoons, and one playing the bones (a set of two pieces of ivory that are played like castanets). There was no singing, unlike the other islands, but the place was so mobbed and loud that a song would have gone unheard in any case.

The *ceili* in the Parish Hall was as crowded as the bar, and the dancing was not as good as on Inishmore, perhaps because of all the celebrating that was done before it. I stayed just a short time, for it had begun to rain and I had a long walk to my lodging.

The unpredictability of the weather here adds to the charm of the islands, and the sun burst forth the following morning, making a crystal of the sea in its reflection.

There are many ruins on this island worth visiting, and I spent the day searching them out. O'Brien's Castle, a fourteenth- or fifteenth-century fort, sits on the highest point of the island, and from there a clear and beautiful view is presented of the other islands and of the formidable Cliffs of Moher in County Clare. The O'Briens were defeated by the "ferocious O'Flahertys" in 1585 over possession of the islands, which explains the pervasive presence of the Flaherty name here. In 1652 the Cromwellian invaders from England destroyed the fort, but it had taken them a full year to conquer the Aran Islands after the conquest of Galway City.

I ended the day at a sunken church called Teampall Chaomháin, the church of St. Cavan, where centuries of blown sand had covered it nearly to the gable tops. It has a small nave and chancel, and after climbing down into it I said a few prayers in Latin that I had remembered from my altar-boy youth. It seemed the thing to do when buried in time.

On top of the graveyard where this church lies deep in the ground are many old engraved slabs and Celtic crosses. I sat there for a while and watched a great storm cloud approaching. It appeared suddenly as from a Druid's wand, and with it came a hard breeze. I thought of outrunning it to Mrs. Conneely's house, but the blues and grays of the imminent sky were too overpowering a sight. The town before me, An Baile Thíos, seemed frozen in acrylic, and I sat there willing to be wet.

The storm passed over, and broke, I suppose, over the Burren in County Clare.

In the evening I went to the bar just a short distance from my lodging house. It is owned by Mrs. Conneely's brother-in-law Thomas. There were few people at the bar, and the conversation was shared by all.

Thomas Conneely, it turned out, had been a friend of the Irish writer Brendan Behan, who had come to this island to sharpen his use of the Irish language and to write *Borstal Boy*. Behan also spent some time on Inishmore, and a man at the bar told the following story about him.

"Brendan Behan was in Kilronen on the Big Island, and he was doing his usual bit of drinking and having a good time. Well, there was a *garda* [police] sergeant there who though Brendan was making a public nuisance and told him that he would summons him if he found him drunk again. In those days if a man was summonsed, he would have to make his own way to a judge in Galway, a trip that took some of them weeks to make. Well, one Saturday night Brendan was drunk and the sergeant was going to summons him, but then thought better of it. He decided he would send Brendan to church instead. So he said to Brendan, "Do you believe in God?

"'I do,' Brendan said.

"'Do you believe in the Blessed Virgin Mary?' asked the sergeant.

"'Ah, I do,' replied Brendan, 'and in the assumption of Herself in Heaven, and in the Resurrection. I believe it all except for the stuff that they're saying about that Matt Talbot.'

"Now Blessed Matt Talbot from the Dublin working class is now on his way to sainthood, and Brendan just couldn't believe that a saint could grow out of the Dublin working class he knew.

"The sergeant let the small heresy pass and ordered Brendan to mass the next morning. Well, Brendan arrived early at the church and took over the job of escorting people to the pews. He left the front pew open until the sergeant and his family came to the church, and after shaking the sergeant's hand and wishing him the best of the day and of religion, he escorted the sergeant and his family to the front pew. Well, the sergeant was imprisoned there and couldn't walk around to keep an eye on Brendan, so Brendan skipped out and ran to the bar and hammered on the door until someone opened it to give him a drink."

Afterward, I played two tunes on the tin whistle, and an old man of the intense, intransigent type applauded vigorously when I finished. It would be a grave mistake, I thought, to take the stern nature of these people for arrogance.

I arose early the next morning, wrote a little in my notebook, and after thanking Mrs. Conneely for her kindness I made my way to the air strip and the plane that would return me to Inishmore.

The flight took just a few minutes, but in that short time the view of the islands, *dúns*, castles, and ruined churches was magnificent.

Mrs. O'Flaherty hugged me on my return and asked if she could feed me since I arrived after the dinner hour. I wanted only a bath, and Mrs. O'Flaherty made a coal fire to heat the water for me.

In the evening I went to the Parish Hall *ceili* with Máirtín and, at his suggestion danced with a very pretty young woman. She smiled at my approach, but again, after hearing my American accent became disappointed, and the dance became a kind of ordeal for both of us. The *ceili* was not as vibrant and life-filled as the last I attended here, and I was told that it was because there were so many visitors at this one, much more than at the other. There seems to be a direct relationship between the amount of visitors on Inishmore and the degree of happiness and relaxation of the islanders. There people are different from the rest of Ireland's people, in that they are less outgoing and more introverted although Mrs. O'Flaherty was certainly an exception to the generalization. I felt myself the intruder at the *ceili*, in much the same way I've felt when going into a bar for cigarettes in the now largely black South Bronx, though the faces on Inishmore are white, the blood and heritage the same as mine.

At the same time, I felt a great affinity for the people of the Aran Islands. They had a history of hardship, of separateness. For generations they were thought of as ignorant and savage by the English-speaking people of Galway and, according to the stories I've heard, were much discriminated against in Galway City. Now the flow of traffic has turned around, and more mainlanders go to the islands than islanders to the mainland. Perhaps the islanders have some justification for their aloofness, for no group of people can happily withstand a constant stream of tourists who come to fulfill an image rather than experience and understand a place. It is probable that each islander has at some time or other suffered some rudeness or lack of consideration from visitors, and therefore has developed the defense of exclusiveness.

There are, as near as I can tell, three groups of people on this island: the native Irish-speakers, the visiting Irish-speakers, and the visiting non-Irish-speakers. My anti-American friend from my earlier visit to Inishmore, the young teacher from Drogheda, belonged to the second group; he told me that he too felt the exclusivity of the islanders, a feeling he'd not had in other *Gaeltacht* areas. At the *ceili* tonight he danced with only the Irish-speaking young women who were visiting. Although he remarked on the good looks of the island women, he would not ask them to dance, for, as he said, it might lead to unnecessary trouble with the island men.

All the island men have, at one and the same time, a unique servantlike gentleness and a repressed violence, an intimidating combination that shows very much in the intensity of their gaze. In his book about the islands, Synge said "[the] grief of the keen . . . seems to contain the whole passionate rage that lurks somewhere in every native of the island." Now that the keening is gone, perhaps the "passionate rage" is released through the wild dancing that borders on violence and the hard, intimidating playfulness that coexists with the dancing. The young men constantly roughhouse in a brutal way by punching each other hard in the chest, but I did not see any actual fistfights while I was there, although my friend from Drogheda told me he saw two—one involving a glass that was dramatically broken on the bar.

After the *ceili* I saw Máirtin go off with a young woman, walking down the road into complete darkness. Though I was wearing a heavy Aran sweater, I shivered with the cold, wondering where a courting young man and a young woman could go on this island of rocks to escape the night air. Some of the young men have motor scooters, and I noticed that only the prettiest girls and young women rode behind them as the crowd went off after the *ceili*. The status of a new car among young adults in America is not much different.

A small red van, the nearest thing to a bus on the island, came, and along with fifteen others, I crowded into it. Mrs. O'Flaherty's sixteen-year-old hired girl Julia sat on my lap. She was very shy—hardly ever talked— but I suspect that was because one of her front teeth was missing. It seems all but a lucky few are affected by the lack of good dentistry on the Aran Islands. Anthropologists in the future, I thought, would be able to develop human economic groupings by studying dental remains.

The morning brought heavy and constant rain, and I decided at breakfast to walk in it. I maneuvered around the deeper puddles in the road to the rock steps by the beach, but when I arrived there I looked as if I had been walking in the surf. I sat for only a few minutes, trying to determine if it was the rain or the ocean spray that was pelting my face. I would have stayed longer had the temperature been higher. This rain and this wind-carried surf are fundamental to the beauty of Aran—the rugged splashing on the rocks is life's metaphor there.

Back at Mrs. O'Flaherty's I dried myself and sat back on the bed by the window overlooking the dim Connemara hills, listened to the rain's rhythm, and read the afternoon long. Toward evening I heard the clear sound of a banjo coming from below, and I went down. There I found Mrs. O'Flaherty, Máirtin, the teacher from Drogheda, a young couple from Mallow, in County Cork, two young women from Dublin, and two from Galway City. One of the young women from Galway, Brig, was playing a fast reel on the banjo, her fingers moving up and down the neck as gracefully as a harpist's. She had a charming, generous way about her that to me represents the real Ireland. It was obvious to me that she felt a genuine freedom in all she said and did, the kind of freedom that comes with untried honesty.

We began to sing songs, each one in the room taking a turn which is the Irish way. I sang a satirical song called "Moses Aye-too-ral, Aye-too-ral-aye-a," but when it came around to me again I recited Patrick Pearse's *The Rebel*, a poem of great propaganda power. When I finished, Máirtin said, "It makes you feel you could eat an Englishman," a remark which saddened me, however true the poem was when it was written before 1916. The English have lost in Ireland, and continue to lose in the North, and there is no point in Anglophobia anymore.

Afterward, everyone went down the road to the bar, but I stayed to write under the gaslight.

The rain was still falling the following day. At breakfast I asked the teacher from Drogheda his opinion on the north, knowing that he had read the radical literature of black revolutionists, and thinking he would be supportive of the Irish Republican Army (IRA) Provisional position. He was not. He told me that he believed in a united socialist Ireland, but that there was no justification at all for the bombings and the killing of innocents. His positions seemed not much different from those of most of the people I'd met in Ireland.

I decided to walk again to Dún Aengus, and on the road I met Brig. I asked for her thoughts on the North, and she told me that it didn't seem a part of her world. She worked for the government tax office, spoke fluent Irish, knew traditional music, and spent all of her holidays in *Gaeltacht* areas; yet this young woman with such an Irish consciousness felt removed from the turmoil of the North, as if it wasn't Irish.

We parted at the Kilmurvey cemetery, for I decided to sit on an old tombstone and watch the waves dance, rather than climb the rocky path of Dún Aengus.

While there I thought of the father of one of four young girls who had come a few years ago from Belfast to march in a St. Patrick's Day parade in New York City. The girls lived with my family and me for two weeks, and so when we came to Ireland later I asked them to spend a day with us in Dublin. It was then that I met the father, a man I will call Desmond, for he had escorted them south to the Republic.

Up until three years before, Desmond had had a steady job, but he now lived on the dole, or welfare, as it is called in the United States. He had been gunned down in the street, from behind, by unknown assailants, and six bullets lodged in his body. He was a quiet husband and father and did not appear to have even a marginal temper. He was shot, he thought, by Protestant extremists because his sons were involved with the IRA. Just months before that shooting, his eldest son had been shot dead. Not long after that his younger son was caught after a bank robbery and sent to Long Kesh for eight years. Desmond had been bombarded with unhappiness, yet he maintained that cool contact with reality that comes with war. He told me that since people in the North were being murdered, one or two a day, a civil war ought to happen where many people are killed and perhaps force a real solution. The deaths will come anyway, he told me.

After thirteen innocents were killed by British soldiers in Derry (Londonderry), on January 30, 1972, what is called "Bloody Sunday," a crowd collected in front of the British Embassy on St. Stephen's Green in Dublin. There they stayed for three days, an emotional need for revenge or retaliation growing with each passing hour. The English officials removed all their files and valuables for they foresaw in the faces of the Dubliners what was to come. On the third day the crowd burned the Embassy. It had to be done, I was told by a reasonable man, to appease the anger and placate the old hatred that was finding rebirth. If British soldiers had killed another thirteen the following week, he said, the Irish of the Republic would have demanded a declaration of war or something as harsh. The reaction in Ireland would have been beyond the point of placation and a resolution condemning Britain certainly would have been demanded, perhaps within the United Nations. But it did not happen, and the politicians in London, Northern Ireland, and the Republic continue to seek a political solution to which all parties are amenable. Another two thousand or so people have been killed in the meantime. This, I think, is what makes a calm, peace-loving man like Desmond advocate a bloody civil war.

The next day, my last full day on the Aran Islands, Mrs. O'Flaherty arranged for me to meet Maggie Dirrane, the woman in Robert Flaherty's film *Man of Aran.* I remembered her clearly from the film, standing tall and straight, carrying a basket of seaweed, her face—the epitome of the unique wide-cheeked, small-mouthed Aran beauty—strong against the wind, her long Aran dress swept close against her firm body. She was a great beauty—there are still great beauties on these islands—and the vision of her strong determination and bucolic naturalness had been fixed within me since the first time I saw the film. *Man of Aran* has become a classic documentary, and so Maggie Dirrane will live forever in the history of cinema.

A man named Dan came to pick us up in a small car. Dan was a big man and powerful looking, but shy and deferential. He seldom completed a sentence in my presence without the word "sir," which can be disarming for a New Yorker. We set off towards the northwest end of the island, to a village called Onacht.

After passing a group of seventh-century ruins called the Seven Churches, we came to Maggie's house—a small, whitewashed, thatched-roof cottage. All the old cottages here have two entry doors, one on the west and one on the east, and Maggie greeted us at the east door, the one facing Connemara. She was a tall woman, then seventy-six, and was wearing an ankle-length black skirt and a matted red woolen sweater. Her face was much wrinkled and most of her teeth were missing, but her memorable blue eyes danced with the liveliness of youth and that even though she was half blind.

Mrs. O'Flaherty introduced us, and thereupon Maggie threw her arms around me, hugging me tight, then held my face in her hands, messed my hair some, and hugged me again, saying all the while that I was "such a handsome boy." I was just a little embarrassed by that, but then completely bowled over when she asked, "Do you like women?" I stumbled over an affirmative answer, and then Maggie hugged me again. It was a reception that pleased me much, for the image of her as a young woman was constant. She and Mrs. O'Flaherty were having a great laugh about it, and then I laughed, too, saying, "If I were just a little older, Maggie, or you a little younger, we would both be in a lot of trouble." We then sat by the open fireplace to talk.

Maggie's was the only house I've been in on Inishmore that did not have a coal stove built into the area of the old hearth. She still used the open fire to heat the place, but there was no fire burning as we sat, although the day was winter cold. Maggie said that she never made a fire before five o'clock.

Maggie's next-door neighbor, who is Mrs. O'Flaherty's sister-in-law, came in and sat for a few minutes. Then, evidently feeling the cold, she and Mrs. O'Flaherty went next door for a cup of tea.

I asked how Flaherty came to choose her for the lead feminine role, and she answered:

"It was over thirty-eight years ago. I was walking to Kilronan one morning, that is, about six miles from where I lived in Kilmurvey. We were very poor, and I had five children then. I passed where Peador Mullin was living, and said hello to him.† I went to Kilronan and did something there, and began to walk back. There were only three sidecars [horse traps] on this island then, and Peador Mullin was putting one to his horse. I said hello again, and walked past. Mr. Flaherty was standing in the doorway of the house and told Peador to call me back. He did call me, but I told him that I had to be home to the children and could pass no time. Peador said then that he would drive me home and that I could have a few minutes. I met Mr. Flaherty, and he asked if he could take pictures of me. He took some pictures and then paid me for the time, do you see, a few shillin's, but that would be what ten pounds is today.

"Then a few days later, Robert Flaherty and his wife and his brother and also Peador came to my house because they wanted to take more pictures. Mrs. Flaherty watched the children as they took the pictures. They paid me again and then left. A few days later Mr. Flaherty and his wife came back, and he told me he wanted me to act in the picture he was going to make. I was very happy, for Mr. Flaherty was such a good man, and I liked him."

Everyone I talked to on the island who knew or had met Robert Flaherty said that he was a good man and that they had liked him. The Aran people, by the way,

---

† Pat Mullen, known to everyone on Inishmore as "Peador," wrote a book called *Man of Aran*, about the making of the film; it was published in the United States by Dutton in 1935.

used the work "like" as we use "love" in America, to voice a strong approval. The film maker evidently was very considerate of the islanders and paid them more than they expected. Mrs. O'Flaherty, who cooked for the crew, told me she earned enough to finance the house I was living in, and Maggie paid for the house she lived in with her earnings.

I talked to Maggie for an hour or so, and she told me how she was nearly taken by the ocean during one of the sequences and of the hazards of filming near the edge of the three-hundred-foot cliffs at Dún Aengus. "I wouldn't do it today," she said. "I'd be too afraid to do those things."

The sky is constantly dark and threatening in the film, if in fact it isn't storming. Maggie told how they would wait through days of sunshine for the appropriately black or stormy day. In that sense, *Man of Aran* is not a documentary as we think of one today—as, for instance, a Frederick Wiseman film is—but a film designed to show the reality of daily hardship as it was in the Aran Islands a hundred years ago. It is a historical documentary.

Maggie told me how she had traveled to New York and Boston and London for the film's openings and how well she was treated by everyone, although she was constantly "lonely for the children" and did not have a happy time of it. Someone asked her to go to California for a screen test there, but she refused because she did not want to be any longer away from her children.

One of her daughters died on her twenty-first birthday from tuberculosis, although Maggie could not bring herself to say the name of that traditionally dreaded disease in wet Ireland and said her daughter had a "spot on the lung." With a sudden sadness, Maggie stared into the dark, empty fireplace and said, "She was a lovely girl, a good girl, but she was not good enough for her God, and she died."

Afterward, Mrs. O'Flaherty and I drove with Dan past the old village of Bun Gabhla to the north tip of the island, which is a geological wonder of small round stones, most not bigger than twelve inches in diameter. The south end of the island is made of high formidable cliffs, but here there is only the washing sea and a flat expanse of loose stones for as far as the land went. On the horizon we could see men fishing from a curragh on the unsettled sea, and Mrs. O'Flaherty showed me where Maggie was nearly drowned during the filming.

Traditionally, the people of Aran Islands have had a profound and superstitious respect for the water surrounding them. I had heard that until recently the islanders refused to learn how to swim and also that if a man fell into the water from a curragh there would be no movement to help him. I asked Mrs. O'Flaherty if that was true, and she replied "Yes, it is. I heard that as a child. And the corpses too. If men were in a curragh and saw a corpse in the water they would not try to get it. It would be let along to find its own resting place."

Next we went back to the Seven Churches—actually, there are remains of only two churches and several buildings of the medieval period. The name "Seven Churches" is erroneously applied to many of Ireland's old monastic centers, such as Glendalough, in County Wicklow, and Clonmacnois, in County Offaly, having to do no doubt with the seven churches of Asia in the Book of the Apocalypse. There is a narrow chancel window about six inches wide and six feet high in the church called Teampall Bhreacáin, and Mrs. O'Flaherty told how as a child she and her friends would climb up on the altar and slip through the window, an adventure that was said to bring good luck. Mrs. O'Flaherty then climbed atop the heavy stone altar to show us how, which was entertaining enough, but when she jumped down from the altar, which is over four feet from the ground, I was concerned for her safety and told her that people ought to be more safety-conscious when climbing altars, to which she replied, *"Wisha!"*

Dan then drove us to Kilmurvey to see a pre-Christian beehive dwelling. Dan waited in the car as we walked along a narrow dirt road, bordered on both sides by nose-high rock walls. It seemed a labyrinth with wall-bordered trails leading off to small fields every hundred yards or so, and we were soon lost. We walked to the sea, and then for about a mile over egg-sized rocks thrown up like sand on a beach, toward where Mrs. O'Flaherty thought the beehive dwelling was. We passed a few stone kilns where the kelp, a source of iodine, used to be made by burning seaweed, two old and abandoned stone huts, and a young girl collecting mollusk shells, but the beehive dwelling was nowhere in sight. It was getting late, and Mrs. O'Flaherty had to be back for high tea and her lodgers, so we abandoned the search. On the way back to the road and Dan's car, we found a sign pointing the way to the beehive dwelling, the sign we had missed partly because of the fading light but more because of the constant talk we engaged in while walking down to the sea. Mrs. O'Flaherty exacted a promise from me then that I would return and that she would be my escort to the famous beehive dwelling. She was such a naturally kind and happy woman. I knew I would miss her.

The next morning I sat by the coal stove waiting for Dan to call for me with his car for the drive to the airfield. It seemed appropriate that I left these islands by airplane. I had come here, filled with romantic expectations, rolling over the rough sea, as Synge came at the turn of the century, and I would leave by a modern contrivance with a new understanding of the changes that modernity forced here. Synge wrote, in *The Aran Islands*:

It is likely that much of the intelligence and charm of these people is due to the absence of any division of labor, and to the correspondingly wide development of each individual, whose varied knowledge and skill necessitates a considerable activity of mind. Each man can speak two languages. He is a skilled fisherman, and can manage a curragh with extraordinary nerve and dexterity. He can farm simply, burn kelp, cut out pampooties, mend nets, build and thatch a house, and make a cradle or a coffin. His work changes with the seasons in a way that keeps him free from the dulness that comes to people who have always the same occupation. The danger of this life on the sea gives him the alertness of the primitive hunter, and the long nights he spends fishing in his curragh bring him some of the emotions that are thought peculiar to men who have lived with the arts.

Synge was a romantic who came to these islands at the suggestion of Yeats and Lady Gregory, bent upon creating a peasant literature. All life has greatly changed since his time, the most significant change being the fact that we don't think of anyone as being a "peasant" anymore in Ireland. I have been among a people in the Aran Islands who have had schooling advantages and opportunities for higher education similar to mine and who come from an economic grouping not much different from the one I came from. I have seen the intelligence, and the charm, of many of the people on the Aran Islands, but I could not, as Synge did, generalize the two attributes to all the islanders. It is fair to say that a division of labor now exists, certainly on the Big Island and to a lesser extent on the smaller islands. Modernity and tourism have brought new sources of income so that people can supplement their government subsidies by driving horse traps, running boarding houses, and otherwise servicing the tourists. Things like cradles and coffins are now brought on the boat from Galway, as are tools, canned goods, fresh food, so the old "varied knowledge and skills" have greatly diminished. While all islanders speak two languages, which would indicate a considerable activity of mind, the exclusivity and sometime pomposity of the use of the Irish language seem to me to be unnecessarily isolating and therefore stifling.

The fishing that is done by the men on the Big Island is done from large lobster boats that travel the whole length of Ireland's south coast; I saw only a few fishermen's curraghs on the water while on Inishmore. On Inishmaan the curraghs are used less for fishing, which is in fact uneconomical from the small craft, than for rowing passengers to and from the *Naomh Eanna* for a small fee each way.

Kelp making is still done here by a few, but it is no longer a major activity of the islanders, for there is little profit in it considering the work involved. Pampooties are hardly worn anymore and so are rarely made. Nets are no longer needed since the fishing is for lobster, which are caught in traps. Thatching is still done, but most of the houses now have tile roofs.

The mental alertness once due to the diversity of work seems to have all but disappeared, and the emotions that Synge said were thought peculiar to men of the arts now result in what would in Alaska be called "cabin fever." It is this lack of diversity in their lives, I think, that prompts the islanders to swing so wildly and carelessly at a *ceili*.

The Aran Islands have had a hard past and have a troubled present, but there are people like Mrs. O'Flaherty, Gregory Connelly, Gobnait, and Sean Faherty who understand the present and are working to secure the future.

The islands have been the subject of a few films and many books, but it could be said they belong to the world because of one classic documentary and one classic diary. Yet Flaherty's dark, almost savage film of a constantly struggling family and Synge's romantic, ethnological journal offer aesthetically pure but incomplete portrayals of life on the Aran Islands.

Perhaps there is a place for each of us where the heart beats in harmony with the mind's music, and perhaps, too, Flaherty and Synge found on the Aran Islands emotional support for the thoughts they brought with them. I came to the islands with a clear vision of the artists' images rooted in my expectations. I also came with an understanding of solipsism. I have been caught up in the moments of exhilaration, of charm, and of admiration among the people of the Aran Islands, but a changing civilization has brought with it its rubbish, dropped along the roads and at ancient monuments, and I have tried to remember that too.

When Synge was here, and Flaherty, the people of the Aran Islands perceived two worlds, theirs and another, both separate and viable. But life on the islands is no longer self-contained, and with electricity it must now be influenced each day by the currents of the larger world. Even the Aran fishermen are controlled by the European Economic Community (the Common Market). And so the isolation diminishes even more.

Aran has greatly changed since the days when Synge could feel those forces of a pure and unaffected native culture which inspired him to create art. Yet there is still a mysterious magnetism here, interwoven with the rain and the wind, the interminable rocks, and the intensity of the people. One can experience on this unique Aran an utter aloneness without alienation, a sense of its history and the courage of its people, and its Celtic magic folded within the limestone of ages. It is the first place I had ever been that generated in me a vow to return and so lessened the sadness upon leaving.

Dan came, and I kissed and hugged Mrs. O'Flaherty. We drove in silence to the grassy field at Killeany where the airplane was waiting.

The car stopped, and I asked Dan the cost.

"Whatever you think it's worth, sir," he said.

I thought about the Aran Islands and realized I would never have that much.

I came here, like the multitudes since Synge and Flaherty, to be a part of the isolation, to be one with the struggles of the wind and the rain and the surging sea. I came as a romantic to a self-created image.

Much had changed. The Big Island was now a holiday camp for foreign tourists, a respite for an emerging Irish middle class, and, for a few, a place of work. The East Island seemed to exist solely for the support and maintenance of a *Gaeltacht* school for Irish-speakers, a summer's challenge to the songs of students. The Middle Island alone was consonant with the romantic vision.

Much will change still.

Yet, in the air heading toward Galway, a wide view of these three small but formidable islands below, the realization occurred that this trip had somehow transformed me, that I was a different person because of it. Instead of t-shirts or post cards or prayer beads, I had come back from this pilgrimage with a strange willingness to slow the pace of my life. I had learned how to be sedentary and calm in the shadow of dark skies before an angry ocean. I will remember always that there is a sea-washed rock shelf waiting in a moist wind for the pilgrims of the world who grow restless. For them, for me, there will always be the Aran Islands, there to wrap the arms of history and solitude around us to make us warm, perhaps even secure, and there will always be a Mrs. O'Flaherty there to give us some tongue and to remind us of what quality there is to life.

ARAN ISLANDS

The intemperate sea of Aran washes the shallow-water stones of Inishmaan—as intemperate as it is here, as intemperate as it always has been.

The fortress of Dún Aengus on Inishmore sits in formidable defiance three hundred feet above the sea. When Sir William Wilde, an eye surgeon and amateur archaeologist (and father of Oscar Wilde), visited this very spot in 1857, he lectured a group of visitors from the British Association: "Now why have I brought you here, and more particularly to the spot where I stand at this moment to address you? It is because after all you have seen, I believe I now point to the stronghold prepared as the last standing place of the Firbolg Aborigines of Ireland, to fight their last battle if driven to the western surge, or as I have already pointed out to you, to take a fearful and eternal departure from the rocks they had contested foot by foot."

Looking west from Dún Aengus at the cliffs of Inishmore, the observer can see the fierce sea climbing nearly three hundred feet up the battered ridges. It was in this kind of weather during the making of Robert Flaherty's film *Man of Aran* that a curragh tried to make shore just beyond these ridges, but fortunately for them the curraghmen were blown out to sea, landing finally at Salthill near the city of Galway. The unpredictable winds had pushed and beaten them a distance of thirty-five miles, the men fighting every yard for survival. But they lived through it. Had the wind pushed them toward the rocks of Aran, it would have been the end.

A stone lying by itself might move a geologist's adrenaline, but for most of us a single stone is unnoteworthy, perhaps even boring. When, though, stones are piled one on another and, as here, given shape as walls or fortresses, they take on another meaning—a dark, moribund reminder of the toilsome past, of the survival battles of our ancestors.

Each stone is a man's effort in lifting, carrying, and placing. So many stones, so much lifting. The count is endless, the labor awesome.

Strange juxtapositions can be found on Inishmore—a tractor riding over hand-made soil that was manufactured by mixing crushed rock with sand and seaweed; a donkey being pulled by the reins by a boy on a motorcycle; a modern house seen through a doorway that was built before Christ was born.

The *chevaux-de-frise* surrounding the middle rampart of
Dún Aengus is as much an obstacle today as it must
have been for ancient invaders. Most of the sharp-
edged stones are the size of a man. One cannot simply
pass over them. They must be climbed, inch by inch.
[I was reminded by them of the pass at Thermopylae,
for just twenty hammer-and-pike throwing Celts
standing on the middle ramparts here could stop an
army.]

How the imagination of youth must work in this
isolation. I saw a young girl on the rock-studded path
to the hillcrest of Dún Aengus. She was carrying a
book and skipped by me with the lightness of a
warming breeze. Would she read the afternoon away,
I wondered, in the shadow of the old fortress? Or
would she simply look out to the end of the rough
ocean and see puff-dreams of Pocahontas, or Maid
Marian, or Juliet? Or, perhaps, would she see
Cuchulain beating back the sea with his fists?

The schoolhouse near Kilmurvey, one of two on
Inishmore, and part of its student body of twenty. It
is a traditional one-room school, grades one to six.
After graduation the students go to an Irish-speaking
boarding school in Galway, on the mainland, where
the larger world begins to intrude on the values of an
isolated society. Many choose not to return to the
islands and make their lives where employment can be
found, on mainland Ireland, in England, or in the
United States.

The Aran Islands do not belong to some misty, romantic notion tied to the memory of John Millington Synge or Robert Flaherty, but to the Aran people, who must determine their own economic and cultural future.

As there are stars in the sky there are silver-gray stones on Inishmore.

It is extraordinary on the islands to see wildflowers
popping up in the unlikeliest places—in limestone
folds, in castle shadows, between sea-thrown boulders.
Here a lone intruder breaks into a cluster of flowers
near Mrs. O'Flaherty's house on Inishmore.

Although their climate is more consistently mild than that of the rest of Ireland, the Aran Islands are often victimized by sudden, violent turns of weather. Often, in winter, the islands become weatherbound for up to three weeks at a time and the people are left in complete isolation. The sea and the wind together make misty, glistening jewels of the islands, impenetrable to ship or plane, and during these storms the Aran people are forcefully reminded of the ageless and closed nature of their society. Storms, though, are no match for electronic transmissions, and soon the multitudinous dots of television will pass through the wind and the rain to invade a culture that has been made distinct by its isolation.

As there are storms to consider on Aran, there is also the pristine air. Though "pristine" is a word that rarely explains, it comes alive here. There are days on Aran when the air is so pure and untainted that I can imagine I can see clear to the Bronx.

On my last day on Inishmore, Mrs. O'Flaherty
arranged for me to meet Maggie Dirrane, the woman
in Robert Flaherty's film *Man of Aran*. I remember her
clearly from the film, standing tall and straight,
carrying a basket of seaweed, her face—the epitome of
the unique wide-cheeked, small-mouthed Aran
beauty—strong against the wind, her long Aran dress
swept close against her firm body. She was a great
beauty—there are great beauties on these islands—and
the vision of her strong determination and bucolic
naturalness had been fixed within me since the first
time I saw the film. *Man of Aran* has become a classic
documentary and so Maggie Dirrane will live forever
in the history of cinema.

A graveyard on Inishmore.

I asked Mrs. O'Flaherty if keening, a unique ritual of wailing over the dead, was still done on the Aran Islands. This is what she said: "No, and isn't it a shame, for I liked it very much, for the women had such beautiful voices. When I was a girl and they began to stop the keening, I thought they didn't respect their dead no more. I did like it very much, the voices in the Irish prayers were so beautiful. The priests didn't like it and made them stop it. It was about twelve or thirteen years ago I was in the graveyard in Kilronan, and there was an old lady there and she did it, but the priest said something to her and she stopped it. That was the last time I heard it."

Dubh Cathair (Black Fort), on Inishmore's southwest coast, is strewn like a rough necklace across a headland just more than a hundred feet above the sea. Here too, as at Dún Aengus, there is a *chevaux-de-frise,* or *abatis.* Because of the relative sophistication in concept and construction of the *abatis,* the dating of these primitive forts becomes confused. The age of the stones, of course, is irrelevant, and so for dating the antiquarian must rely on artifacts found at the site. A hinged ring of bronze with a cable decoration was found at Dún Aengus a few years ago and dated from the fifth century A.D., but as yet there is no conclusive archaeological evidence for the true age of any *dún* on the lands. It is safest to say that these formidable, awesome structures are very early Christian or perhaps pre-Christian in period.

Mr. O'Flaherty of Aras Bhrid, on Inishmore, pits his potatoes for storage.

The small plot of arable land adjoining the O'Flaherty house, like much of the island on the Arans, was "made" by generation of islanders clearing the underlying limestone surface of boulders, breaking and leveling it with sledge hammers, spreading it with sand from the shoreline, mixed with whatever dirt could be found in rock crevices or under rock walls, overlaying it with seaweed and then another layer of sand, and, finally, sprinkling whatever clay could be found over the mixture. In two or three years the rain and the sun would work their magic and the mixture would become soil, ready for the spade.

On Inishmore I walked along the cliffside, passing a magnificent hole cut out of the rock of a lower ledge. Because of fissuring, a huge and almost perfect rectangle of limestone had dropped into the Atlantic from the ledge, leaving an abyss which at high tide fills with seawater, making of it an Olympic size swimming pool. It is called "The Worm Hole" because of an island myth that says it is inhabited by a sea serpent.

In 1921 the Congested District Board of Ireland purchased the Aran Islands from the absentee Anglo-Irish owner for the sum of £ 13,721 (or less than $70,000 at the then current rate of exchange). Tenant farming then became a dark memory, and the land was distributed at minimal cost among the Aran people.

A fisherman-farmer in pampooties and raw-wool clothing tends to his small furrows to facilitate easy weeding. Seaweed was the traditional nutrient for the soil, but in recent years, artificial fertilizers and pesticides are being used more and more.

Dún Conor, a "stone's throw" from the cottage where Synge lived on Inishmaan, seems in appearance to have risen from the ground in the approximate center of the island. Its walls are fifteen to twenty feet high and twelve to eighteen feet thick. It is to me as much a geological as an historical wonder. This most significant ring fort in all of Ireland, indeed, perhaps in all of Europe, has no recorded history and as yet there has been no serious archaeological work done here.

I saw a man who was planting potatoes in his small patch of a field, bending over, pressing each root firmly into the soft tilled soil with his thumb. After a while, he looked up and saw the boat from Galway making a turn from Inisheer, the East Island. "All in good time," I thought I heard him say before he laid the root sack aside and walked slowly to the end of the island and his curragh.

The curraghmen haven't far to go as they walk
blindly, wearing the curragh, it seems, as a fantastic
black rain hat to the water's edge.

There is just one man on all the islands who still
makes these tar-bellied, beetlelike vessels. He lives on
Inisheer in a house that fronts a strand of bleached
sand, his garden a row of glistening black-velvet boats.

The M.S. *Naomh Eanna* (St. Enda) pulls anchor as the last curragh heads to the shore of Inishmaan. There is no pier on this island, nor on Inisheer, and the islanders transport supplies, mail, animals, and people in these small, smooth-surfaced vessels in the same way they have done since the days the large ships had sails. The *Naomh Eanna* will go from here to the Killeany Bay town of Kilronan on Inishmore, where the water is deep enough to dock her. The coast of County Clare can be seen in the distance.

The population of the Aran Islands has been continually declining, from 3,521 in 1841 to 2,863 in 1901 to 1,496 in 1974. The economic history of the islands seems a roller coaster of good times and bad, but mostly bad. Diminishing economic opportunities make the Arans particularly vulnerable to depopulation, and though the recent growth of tourism has beneficial impact for three months of the year, the population and the economy of the islands will not be static until the fishing and other industries expand to make full use of the people.

Here a lone woman walks a wall-bordered road on Inishmaan.

An islander gathers seaweed on Inishmaan for making kelp.

In 1837 an author wrote that the people of Inishmaan were chiefly fishermen and kelp makers. Labor on the Arans had always been diversified, divided between making and repairing clothes, tools, and equipment and building, fishing, farming, and kelp making. Synge thought that the versatility of the Aran people was fundamental to their intelligence and charm. Yet, if kelp making—the burning of seaweed for its potash and iodine—once flourished on the islands, in the last few decades it has gone the way of the pampootie and embroidered shawl. The demand for potash and iodine fell as nitrates and synthetic antiseptics were discovered, and the time and labor required for making kelp became uneconomical. Just recently, though, the alginic acid in seaweed has been found useful in making medical and cosmetic products, and once again the flickering kiln fires may be seen from time to time breaking into the night on the Aran shores.

The southwestern end of Inishmaan at low tide.

The land slopes gently into the ocean around the island, a physical barrier to all but the smallest of craft, such as a curragh. A man told me that a pier would be built here one day, yet it seems there is little incentive for the government to undertake such a large and expensive project. There is no doubt, though, that a pier would unburden the Aran people from the cumbersome methods used to transport goods, people, and animals from the island.

There are two tractors now on Inishmaan, each having arrived disassembled and brought in piece by piece; wheel by wheel, in the curraghs and reassembled on land. It seems an almost Sisyphyean task without a pier.

Father Kearny gives communion to women on Inishmaan. The men will follow when it is seen that the last woman turns from the altar. There has been little change in Catholic ritual here over the centuries. Though mass is said in Irish and not Latin, the men and the women sit apart from each other, separated by the center aisle of the church.

The Irish are as taken with icons as were the prerevolutionary Russians, and in every Aran home the visitor is reminded of the Deity and saints. On Mrs. Mulkerrins' dining-room wall in her house on Inishmaan, there was a picture of the late Archbishop Fulton Sheen, sent to her by an American relative. On a sideboard Mrs. Mulkerrins herself appropriately joined the saints in watching over her guests.

Mr. Mulkerrins of Inishmaan.

A curragh has strong oars, called in Irish *modjee-raw*, that are bladeless and the same width at each end. Since the light craft glides over the water on its glass-smooth bottom, it needs just a little pull on the oars to set it in motion. There are two to four oarsmen to a curragh; they must move and act, according to one island man, "as if there were one brain only."

Mr. Faherty, of Inishmaan, who usually wears the traditional gray wool (called "bauneen") garb and pampooties, here greets a harsh winter day in a modern windbreaker.

A young woman arriving on Inishmaan is given a lift from the curragh to the land.

There is a great commotion as the ship *Naomh Eanna* anchors off the coast of the two pierless smaller islands and the curraghs go racing to her, sometimes disappearing, momentarily, behind a great wave. There is always a pervasive sense of danger when the men are out on the water, for the ocean is never still, and there is much laughter when they return, heaving the boxes of supplies and lifting the women and children to the dry sand.

The women of Aran are generally tall, with wide cheekbones and alert, piercing eyes. Their role is that of mother, and they take pride in large families. They run the household autocratically, and with the ever bourgeoning importance of tourism they are often the keystone of a family's economics. Still, the Aran woman is quiet and unassuming and carries herself with almost imperial dignity as she walks the rock-filled roads of the islands. Here an Inishmaan woman carries enough peat for the day's fire.

On the ramparts of Dún Conor, a monument to the labor of the ancient Celts, on Inishmaan, I play the pipes; the dirge whistles out to sea like a hymn.

Related directly to the Battle-ax people of the Neolithic period, the Celts began civilizing Central Europe before Hammurabi brought his code of laws to Babylon in 2000 B.C. In the eighth century B.C., when the blind poet Homer was seeing visions of Odysseus and the legendary founders of Rome, Romulus and Remus, were licking the smooth side of the she-wolf, the Celts were already a distinct and viable group, building, inventing, using iron, and creating order. They dominated Europe for seven centuries, developing handsaws, chisels, files, soap, chain armor, horseshoes, plowshares, and flour mills. They flourished until the rise of Rome and the much later rise of Anglo-Saxon England sent them scurrying to the west—to the fields of Brittany, to the hills of Wales, to the appendicle of Cornwall, to the mountains of Scotland, and across the water to the Isle of Man and the rocks of Ireland. Some ended in the Aran Islands, here to begin the never-ending toil of rock carrying.

On top of the graveyard on Inisheer where St.
Cavan's Church lies sunken deep in the ground, I
watched a great storm cloud approaching. It appeared
suddenly, as from a Druid's wand, and with it came a
hard breeze. I thought of outrunning it to Mrs.
Conneely's house, but the blues and grays of the
imminent sky were too overpowering a sight. The
town before me, An Baile Thíos, seemed frozen in
acrylic, and I sat there willing to be wet.

The curraghs, lying between rocks on the sand each evening, have an air of inexplicable tranquillity about them, as if they are truly resting, reaffirming the pervasive peacefulness that is the Arans'.

It is a wondrous thing to watch two curraghmen pull
the oars in concert, as sychronized as the violin bows
of an orchestra. They each pull both oars for a while,
and then, without a signal given, the oars on one side
may go stiffly into the water as they both pull hard on
the other oars to change the craft's direction. It is as
if each wave and each oar stroke had a number and
the maneuvers were written down on paper.

A curragh pulls a cow through the water to the interisland ship, the animal swimming naturally enough, but quietly, too pusillanimous to moo. A hoist is lowered from the deck and tied to a cinch that has been strapped around the animal's belly, and it is lifted out of the water. There is no other way to transport cattle or horses from the smaller islands and the animals are consequently destined, without exception and quite literally, to sink or swim. It must be a greater inconvenience to the island men, I thought, than to the animals, since, without a pier, they are forced to inflict such primitive methods on the animals. I also thought, though, that the whole procedure would make an SPCA official cringe.

119

How to kill time on Inisheer. O'Brien's Castle can be seen in the background.

The entertainment of the *seanchai* (storyteller) has given way to the occupying forces of newspapers, magazines, and radio. And soon, probably, television will become the main force in idle hours. Then the stories of Aengus Og, Manannán Mac Lir, Deirdre, and Cuchulain will no longer come from the lips of men unless they are read aloud from books, and young men will no longer commit to memory the histories and the romances, so they in turn can correct their own sons' recitations.

Still, the people of the Aran Islands live in an oral tradition of a sort for the most part, and when they speak, there always seems to be a young one about, listening.

Some of the rock walls are as tall as basketball players, and sometimes I got the feeling as I passed by that I was missing some significant event, a quiet parade perhaps or a competition between men. It made one long for a ladder or a periscope. Yet, for all that, I knew that there was simply another rock wall behind that rock wall.

The hammer-throw contest on Inisheer.

Once each year, people from Inishmore, Inishmaan, and Doolin (in County Clare) travel by boat or curragh to Inisheer, to watch or take part in games of athletic skill and strength. It is a festive outing for all, a day of merriment.

I watched the crowd move like the sea from one place on the field to another, to where a hammer-throw contest was to take place. They left just a little room for the contestants, and one man lost his stride as he stepped up to heave the thirty-four-pound hammer. The heavy iron went sailing toward the crowd, scattering them like sparks struck from molten steel. Fortunately, no one was hurt, but there was much oohing and aahing before the throng returned to their very same places and revived the danger.

O'Brien's Castle, a fifteenth-century fort, sits on the highest point of Inisheer, and from here a clear and beautiful view is presented of the other islands and of the formidable Cliffs of Moher in Country Clare. The O'Briens were defeated by the "ferocious O'Flahertys" in 1585 over possession of the islands, which explains the pervasive presence of the Flaherty name here. In 1652 the Cromwellian invaders from England destroyed the fort in one battle, but it had taken them a full year to conquer the Aran Islands.

The sunken church of Teampall Chaomhain, the church of St. Cavan, on Inisheer, where centuries of blown sand had covered it nearly to the gable tops. It has a small nave and chancel, and after climbing down into it I said a few prayers in Latin that I had remembered from my altar-boy youth. It seemed the thing to do when buried in time.

An islander walks through his field on Inisheer.

An Aran family might own two, five, or more patches of land in various parts of its island. One patch of a holding might be miles from another, and to tend his animals or his crops the Aranman enters a labyrinth of rock walls each day. There are no gates between the walls, and one usually has to disassemble and then rebuild each wall when going from patch to patch.

Looking over the island from a high point on the road to Inisheer's post office, I sensed that everything had become part of a grand and ancient scheme of architecture. The people, the dwellings, the animals, a small patch of sand—everything—seemed to have been carefully placed into position by a very old and very wise environmentalist.

The *ceili* at the Parish Hall on Inisheer. I found the dancing here less wild than the dancing I saw at Inishmore, yet, I though to myself, I would rather be in a fire than dance in my moccasins on any Aran Island dance floor.

These Inisheer striations in a limestone field were
created through millennia of chemical solution by
underground streams and the rain's runoff.

There is a legend, supported by some geological
evidence, that the Aran Islands are all that remains of
a land mass that once joined the Burren limestone of
County Clare to the east and the granite of
Connemara to the north, a land mass that rose in
elevation as it went westward. It is a neat hypothesis,
for the highest point on Inisheer is two hundred feet,
on Inishmaan nearly three hundred feet, and on
Inishmore four hundred feet. On each island there
are enough foldings, bedding jointings, and
conglomerates of granite, feldspar crystals, and fossil-
filled limestone to excite even the most dispassionate
geologist.

137

The Sacred Heart of Mary watched over the sleepers
in Mrs. Conneely's guest room on Inisheer, to placate,
I thought, whatever animadversions regarding the
wallpaper that might exist in the guest's mind. Still,
the rich texture of the bedspread was as comforting as
any I'd slept under, and a night on the Aran Islands
did not pass that I didn't sleep as soundly as I ever
had in my life.

There is a mysterious magnetism here, interwoven
with the rain and the wind, the interminable rocks,
and the intensity of the people. One can experience
on these unique Aran Islands an utter aloneness
without alienation, a sense of its history and the
courage of its people, and its Celtic magic folded
within the limestone of ages. It was the first place I
had ever seen that generated in me a natural vow to
return and so lessened the sadness upon leaving.

DENNIS SMITH, himself a first-generation Irish American, is the author of *Final Fire, Firehouse* (with Jill Freedman), *Dennis Smith's History of Firefighting in America,* the best-selling *Report from Engine Co. 82,* and, most recently, *Glitter and Ash. The Aran Islands: A Personal Journey* has grown out of the author's lifelong interest in Irish literature in general and the writings of John Millington Synge in particular.

BILL POWERS is staff photographer and art director for Criminal Justice Publications. His photos have appeared in numerous books and magazines, and he has published two short novels for young people, *The Weekend* and *A Test of Love.*